SAVANNAH DOGS II

SAVANNAH DOGS II

MINNIE MCQUILLEN BEIL
EDITOR

FREDERIC C. BEIL

SAVANNAH

TO

OUR AGENCIES

Humane Society of Chatham–Savannah
Pet Assistance League of Savannah
Save-A-Life Animal Welfare Agency
Second Chance Dog Rescue and Referral

AND OUR

DOCTORS OF VETERINARIAN MEDICINE

Debbie Barrett
Melanie Bevere
Richard W. Bink
Patrick Bremer
Daniel Brogdon
Al Camacho
Jerry L. Case
Kyle Christiansen
Ernest Compton
Max M. Cooper
Deanna Douglas
James E. Ducey
Pamela Fandrich
Christopher Gall
Kim Gasser
Heather Gill
Alan C. Gross
Julie Harelson
Stephanie Hazlett
Don H. Howard
David Howes
G. Scott Hudspeth
J. Patrick Hudspeth
Karen Kane

David B. Kicklighter
J. Stanley Lester
Deana Livingston
Carla Case McCorvey
Lesley Y. Mailler
Edward Marion
Steven M. Marlay
Beth Martin
Peter Winn Martin
Joe Morris
Chad Nance
Rachel Peeples
Robert Pernell
George Runnals
Billy C. Sanders
Denise Schneider
John D. Schoettle
Twila Seefeldt
Paul Shealy
Terri Sparks
Charra Sweeney-Reeves
Michele Trammell
Donald R. Webb

Therefore to this dog will I,
Tenderly not scornfully,
Render praise and favor:
With my hand upon his head,
Is my benediction said
Therefore and forever.

—Elizabeth Barrett Browning,
To Flush, My Dog

CONTENTS

EDITOR'S NOTE xiii

Annie Cetti 1
Yogi Cetti 3
Niblick Cetti 5
Rosebud Kittle of Tybee 7
Daisy Mae Kittle 9
Niamh Harold 11
OTCH U-OCH Heelalong
Rev Em-Up Spot 14
Chloe Moros 17
Chase Cantey Sprott 19
Spice Cortese 21
Sebastian Martin 24
Penapoli 26
Cassidy Rosengart 28
Vincent II 30
Captain Rhett's Baby Foots 33
Kajah Marrah 35
Toby Brunswick, Jr. 37
Lady 40
Empress Samantha 42
Trixee-Dog Doser 46
Lacey Mikell 48

ix

CONTENTS

Too Cute Oscar Barney Ford 50
Mid-Summer Night's Dream 52
Lady Grace of Piedmont 54
Chauncey Hosking 56
Gypsy Jenkins 59
Ms. Kizy McVicker Jensen 62
Daisy 65
Annabelle Lee Saturday 67
Portia Tucker McLaughlin 69
No Bigger'n a Minute 71
Charlie Barrow 73
Mr. Murphy Morris 75
Chicco and Reilly 78
Lacy Ashley 81
Spottee Ashley 83
Ted-E Salter 85
Bacarde 87
Oscar Noble 89
Bailey 92
Sam Schwartz 94
Precious McNeill Smith 96
Miss Birdie 98
Maggie Watson Karliss 100
Cayenne Pepper Kerkoski 103
Shayna King 105
Easy Michael Ferguson Denham 107
Lyndale M'Lord Riley 110
Hunter, Lord of Whitemarsh 112
Baker 115
Zoe Smith 118
Joey 120

CONTENTS

Roxy Borden 122

Ginger Bovee 125

Greta 127

Hannah Harper 145

Deimos 148

Phobos 151

Tippy Gordon 153

Cid 156

Desi 158

Lady of Savannah 160

Lacey 163

Precious Magnolia 165

Hannah 167

Hamilton Genser 170

Cookie 173

Dazie-Doo 176

Lucky-Dog 178

Junior, the Wonder Dog 181

Mr. Brinkelsworth and Mr. Baileykins 184

Winston Gottlieb 187

Roxie Iocovozzi 189

Chloe 191

Macie 193

Ginger Johnson 195

Abbey Ledesma 197

Bambi Lazzaro 200

Matillda 202

Henry Macbeth 204

Fritz Lee Schlawiner 206

Alex Sheffield 208

Hugo Macdonald 211

CONTENTS

Herschel 213

Mini-me 216

Hope Wolf 219

Molly White 222

Gilhaven's Supernatural D-Lite 225

Cedar Lynn Sweeney-Reeves 228

Darien Sokolowski 230

LA's Gracie Mae 232

Simone Muhlenkamp 235

Bear of Monterey Square 238

Friendly Sussman 242

Bearfoot 244

Sainte Abigail of Savannah 247

Hunter Duckpond Potts 249

Xena the Warrior Princess 252

Simba 254

Blocker's Bridget Claire 259

Scout Murray 261

Godfrey Wayne James 263

Honey DelMonte 265

Blackjack, King of the Deck 268

Dixie Crystal 270

Gladys 271

Guinness 273

Hard-Headed Hannah
the Tramp of Savannah 276

Detective Dirty Harry Callahan 278

Fiona 281

Chloe Beil 284

She Knew What She Liked 287

EDITOR'S NOTE

It is my extraordinary pleasure to bring to you, to the members of your pack, and to people who just love to read about dogs *Savannah Dogs II*, the sequel to my first book, *Savannah Dogs*. Much to my surprise, there were many more dogs who believed that their stories needed to be told; and now that I have their stories, I can assure you that they were right. In these pages you will meet 114 new dogs, all of whom live in Savannah or have some compelling relationship with Savannah, a town that loves her canine residents.

This book also is dedicated to the organizations and veterinarians who provide assistance to dogs-in-need in our community. My acknowledgment and gratitude is extended to them all.

Albert Schweitzer, the theologian, missionary physician, and music scholar, once wrote: "Hear our humble prayer, O God, for our friends, the animals, especially for animals who are suffering; for any that are hunted or lost, or deserted or frightened or hungry; for all that must be put to death. We entreat for them all thy mercy and pity, and for those who deal with them we ask a heart of compassion and gentle hands and kindly words. Make us, ourselves, to be true friends to animals and so to share the blessings of the merciful."

May this collection of dog stories be a sharing of those blessings.

MINNIE MCQUILLEN BEIL

ANNIE CETTI
("ANNIE POOH")

Ah, Savannah in the springtime. There's nothing like it. The azaleas are in full bloom. There are lots of big bumblebees flying around. What does this have to do with a spoiled bulldog? you ask. Well, I'm not like other bulldogs. My name is Annie and I catch bees. No, silly, not with a net, with my mouth.

You see, my human companions did not know at first that I possessed this amazing talent. (I didn't even know.) One day I was smelling the pretty flowers when all of a sudden a bee started buzzing around my head. It was a bit unnerving, that buzz in my ears. So, snap! The bee was gone. I didn't realize that bees could bite back. (Boy, that hurt.) When my companions came home from work, my face was swollen like a balloon. They racked their brains trying to figure out what had happened. (I couldn't speak to explain it to them 'cause my cheeks were too swollen.) They called my doctor, who suggested something called an antihistamine. They brought me in the house and I slept for hours. When I woke up, I felt better and wanted to bee-hunt some more. My human companions were still baffled as to

1

what could have caused this episode. My dog companions, Yogi [see pages 3–4] and Nibby [5–6], were fine, but our humans looked us over head-to-toe and, of course, found nothing. It was several days later, when we were all in the yard playing together, that another bumblebee buzzed my head and I snapped at him. (Those things can be annoying.) It was then that my humans figured out how talented I was. I could catch bees. Other dogs can fetch the ball, roll over, or even shake hands, but not me. Those mundane things do not amuse me. The catching of large-flying insects that sting—now that's a game worth playing.

For the most part I don't catch much. This makes my human companions very happy. You would think that I would have learned my lesson, getting stung a couple of times already. I've only been successful a pawful of times. Still, I try for the thrill of the game and to end that annoying buzzing. Plus, the occasional drug-induced nap is a bonus. My human companions get very nervous in the springtime. For some reason the female one planted some jasmine in the backyard. It's very fragrant and attracts large numbers of bees. Maybe she planted the jasmine just for me. My dog companions have not caught on to my game. They play those mundane games, trying to amuse our humans in more traditional ways. I remain the only one in the family with the distinction of being a "canine bee catcher." Too bad that's not an event at the Doggie Carnival; I could win first prize. Well, there's always the spring to look forward to. Meantime I'll continue to hone my skill. Maybe one day soon I'll catch another bee.

ANNIE

YOGI CETTI ("YOGI MAN")

I'm a basset hound. To most people the words "basset hound" suggest slow, laid back, maybe even lazy, but that's not me. I'm a bundle of boundless energy, not to mention a barrel of laughs.

When I was a puppy, I went to live with a little girl and her family. Her father thought that I would be a good companion for her because I was a basset hound. He bought in to the lazy theory. Little did he know that under those lazy eyes was hiding an endless river of energy ready to overflow. Needless to say, it didn't work out with them. My boundless energy led me away from their home, and I began to explore Wilmington Island.

One day some nice people found me and took me home, where I met their bulldog, Annie [see pages 1–2]. She was big and scary-looking, but I saw right through that. We became fast friends and even room-mates. After I joined the family, my humans adopted Nibby [see pages 5–6], my cocker spaniel friend. I have a feline friend too, but he lives inside. He just stares at me through the sliding glass door. Sometimes I bark at him and pretend I'm hunting, but when they open the door, I just sniff him and tell him "Hello."

I like to amuse my humans with my wild antics. Have you ever seen a basset hound that can catch food in mid-air, run in circles without getting dizzy, and even shake hands? Lazy? I think not.

I have a nice big yard and all the responsibilities that come with it. Several times a day I walk the perimeter to make sure all is well. If I smell anything out of the ordinary, I stop and give a warning bark or two. When my patrol is finished, I like to take a nap. If it's chilly, I find a sunny patch. When it's warm, I like to dig basset-size holes in the dirt, much to my humans' dismay. They fill them in, but while they're at work I dig some more.

One time I decided to nap at the base of an oak tree. I used the root for a pillow, and when I woke up I had a hematoma on my ear! It was traumatic at first, but turned out to be a good thing 'cause I got to go see Dr. Schoettle, my favorite vet. He fixed my ear and then, when we got home, I got to stay inside for a while and also got extra peanut-butter bones.

My greatest love in life is peanut-butter bones. I live for them. My humans keep them in a glass jar on the floor; and when I hear the lid clank, I jump to attention. I'll do anything for a bone.

I know I'm a lucky dog because I found human companions who appreciate my unique basset qualities and don't mind my crazy antics. Sometimes they even encourage and reward me.

YOGI

4

NIBLICK CETTI
("NIBBY")

I'm a lucky dog. You know we canines aren't as street-wise as our furry counterparts, the felines. We don't seem to have as many lives. That's why when my human companions saw me nose-to-nose with the bumper of a pickup truck on Victory Drive, they knew they had to help me.

I was three years old, and my first companions were moving away. When they sold their house, I stayed with the new owners. I don't think they were real keen on me 'cause when I got out one day they didn't go looking for me. I made my way to Victory Drive, and that's when I got lucky. First, because that pickup truck stopped in time. Second, because this nice lady and her husband kept following me. I was skeptical at first and tried to elude them. Finally they opened up some dog food and put it on the sidewalk. I was quite hungry, plus I figured anyone who has dog food in their car must be a dog person. They picked me up and started looking at my necklace with the dangly things on it. I didn't have a name tag, just that silver tag you get after the vet gives you that shot.

The nice people took me for a haircut and to the vet

for my skin problems. The lady was on the phone a lot. She called a county agency, which tracked the tag number to the vet that gave me my last shot. She got in touch with my original human companions, who filled the new people in on my circumstances and asked that they assist in finding me a good home.

The nice people who found me already had four dogs, so they really couldn't keep me, but they knew a lot of people and thought they could find me a good home. They looked for several weeks to find me a new home. They ruled out several potential new companions, until one day they found a man who seemed nice. The lady took me to meet the man. If all went well, I was to go with him to my new home. The lady asked the gentleman several questions, and it appeared he would pass her test, until she asked one last question: "Where will he stay at your house?" The man replied that he planned to let me loose on his property with his other dogs. All of a sudden the nice lady started to cry. She knew from experience that I was not good at finding my way back home. She picked me up in her arms and carried me out of that place. We drove back to the house, the nice lady crying all the way. When we got home her husband gave us a big hug, and I've been with them ever since. That was eight years ago. She has since confided that I stole her heart on the first day when she found me, and that she knew no one else could love me the way she does. That's why I'm one of the lucky dogs.

NIBBY

ROSEBUD
KITTLE
OF TYBEE
("ROSIE")

I was born in Florence, South Carolina, to a large family. When my mom and dad came to visit, they couldn't resist my beautiful markings. It was love at first sight. So now my home is in Savannah. An apple-head Chihuahua, I am black and white with tan eyebrows and have some tan on my legs. I weigh about seven pounds. I am large for my size, but I am still cute. I gained a little bit of weight when my mom had a bad motorcycle accident and was in bed for a couple of months. Those days were great for me. All we did was eat, sleep, and eat some more. I was alone then and my mom was all mine. Now I have a sister, Daisy [see pages 9–10], who is very bossy, but more about her in her story.

Most of my days are spent in Relaxation Therapy. My mom owns the place, so I get to be boss. Daisy was right—all the kids in the mall come to visit me. I share them with Daisy because I have enough love to go all around.

I am afraid of things that move too fast, move too slow, and sometimes of things that don't even move at all. I do a good job at work. I am the great protector and I am so adorable. Lots of love to all of you. Come and see me.

ROSIE

DAISY MAE KITTLE ("DAISY")

It all started a year and a half ago. I was born to a family with two small human children who loved to run around and pound me on the head with their dolls. I was the last of the litter of wolf Chihuahua still at home and had almost given up on finding a new family to adopt. Being easy to get along with and very humble, it was most surprising to me that people were not beating down the door to be mine. My beautiful looks should have been enough on their own to land me into the lap of luxury. With my honey-blonde, brown coat, big bright eyes, and wonderful smile, I usually get my way. But more about that later.

When the day finally came to get a human family, I used a tactic that has worked very well for me ever since. Having learned the best way to get attention was to open my big brown eyes really wide and let my ears droop ever so slightly, I was able to get the attention of my new adoptive parents, Kathy and Bruce. My new sister, Rosebud [see pages 7–8], already lived with them, but I took over as soon as I sauntered into the house. Although Rosebud was a little shy, all it took was a lot of wet kisses and nose nuzzles to get her on my side.

Rosebud is very loving and let's me be the boss, which I like very much. She is black and tan with a white chest and collar and also has big bright eyes. But I am still prettier, I think.

My favorite thing to do is to help mama with the laundry. She takes it out of the machine, which makes laundry warm, and dumps it on the couch. As she folds, I burrow down until all she can see is my perfect little black-nosed snout and big bright eyes looking adoringly at her. She can't help but pick me up and take me to the kitchen for a treat. And she really keeps good treats for Rosebud and myself. Mama is just the best mom in the world.

My other favorite thing to do is greet our clients at our business, Relaxation Therapy. They all love me and Rosebud and sometimes stop by just to see us. Everybody in the mini-mall where we work knows us and gives attention. Kathy thinks that she is the one that they come to see, but Rosebud and I know differently. Come see us.

DAISY

NIAMH HAROLD
("NIAMH THE WEAVE,"
"PRINCESS NIAMH")

I barely remember running around in a backyard near Bacon Park with eleven other "gold-a-dors." My real mother, Josie the golden retriever, was having a tough time dealing with so many pups and was ready to be done with us. I lived under some steps and spent my days rolling in dirt and barking at everything that passed by.

One Friday these strange humans came to meet me. The man, I call "Dad," kept saying, "Aw, come on now. She's cute or at least she will be with some attention. Let's take the black female." Mom wasn't sure she wanted any of us. "That is, without a doubt, the ugliest puppy I ever saw." Her comment did nothing for my already fragile ego. It was not my fault that I was mal-nourished, and had bad teeth and multiple bald spots. In spite of my unsavory appearance, they took me rid-ing in their car and I never looked back.

Mom held me in her lap all the way to Tybee, and I fell madly in love. I kiss her on the mouth whenever possible and talk to her incessantly. She worries about my conversational skills. "Niamh, *what* do you want

11

now? Please help me understand." All I want is to go outside, to come back inside, go outside, come back inside, and go outside again.

About a year ago, Mom came home late. It was dark, and she didn't change clothes like she normally does. We had our kissing and feeding ritual and then she hooked up my brother Pearse [see *Savannah Dogs*, pages 155–57] and me in our "gentle leaders," which are supposed to help us "behave." We were out "doing our business" when it started to drizzle. Since I was crying and grabbing the leash, Mom decided to rush home.

We were heading down the hill into our neighborhood when the "Wiley Gang," an Italian greyhound and two whippets, appeared by the pond. They barked and lunged, and we retaliated. Pearse and I jumped with everything our combined 180 pounds could muster. Mom tried to fly like Peter Pan, but crash-landed on concrete and was tangled in leashes. There was dead silence until nice Pamela yelled, "Are you okay?" I can't repeat Mom's answer. From nowhere, Alice, the mom of Little Bit, Sophie, and Buttercup, the golden girls, grabbed us and pulled Mom off the street.

We bounded home with Alice in charge. Pamela showed up with a car and it was party time. Mom should hold open house every night. Pearse and I had such fun kissing everyone. Pamela drove Mom away, and Alice waited for Dad to come home. Hours later—it seemed like a lifetime—Mom returned. She was pale and smelled funny. I wanted to kiss her, like I always do, but she yelled at me, "*No, Niamh!* Don't do that. You and Pearse already shattered my wrist!" I don't have a clue what she meant. Since then, Pearse and I walk separately, which is no fun; and, when we see the whippets, Mom and Pamela head in opposite directions. In spite of it all, Mom says she loves me and that I'm her special girl who changed from an ugly duckling into a swan.

NIAMH

OTCH U-OCH
HEELALONG
REV-EM-UP
SPOT
("SPOT")

OTCH U-OCH Heelalong Rev-em-up Spot, UDX, TD, OA, OAJ ("Spot" to his friends) has been my partner for more than twelve years. I'm no writer, but since Spot's much too modest to tell about himself, this job falls to me.

Spot is a Border collie, so the fact that he's smart and energetic is hardly surprising. Spot was supposed to be my now ex-husband Bob's dog—a new dog to follow in the footsteps of Brig, the wonderful obedience champion that be was then campaigning. Bob wanted a big, tough Border collie, but Spot turned out smaller than had hoped, and very "soft," a young dog that so hated to make a mistake. Soon it became obvious, even to Bob and me, what had been so clear to all who knew us—Spot was my dog.

And what a dog. Spot loves to play. Any game will do, so I adapted his training to suit his intense play-drive. Every new exercise became a game. He undertood that he won by doing an exercise correctly, thus earning a treat or toy reward. He thrived on the game, and got so good at playing that he soon began earning obedience titles, ultimately earning the title Obedience Champion in two registries.

Meanwhile my marriage had failed, and I depended even more on my relationship with this wonderful dog. Besides being my partner in the ring, Spot was at my side almost constantly. In spite of his active Border collie nature, Spot has always been willing to take the time to allow me a hug, to wash my face with his tongue, or to snuggle close for a nap. During some of the rougher times of my divorce, his beautiful coat absorbed many a tear.

Soon after my divorce, a small growth on Spot turned out to be cancerous and life-threatening. Radical surgery was done to remove all affected tissue. I assumed this would end his athletic career. My goal was to save his life, not necessarily return him to his previously strong stamina. But I didn't consider Spot's determination to "play." Soon after surgery Spot was as sound as ever and eager for new games. During the four years after surgery, he has added a tracking title and also many agility titles, represented by the string of initials accompanying his name.

Spot, however, doesn't care about titles. He just likes to play. At the age of twelve he's finally and reluctantly been retired from competition. He still likes to keep busy and enjoys being demo-dog for my obedience training classes, running through agility courses with the jumps lowered as well as racing through all the tunnels and weave poles with much enthusiasm. We also hope to spend more time tracking (just a fun game of hide-and-seek to Spot) and possibly, if time permits, adding yet one more title, the TDX ("Tracking Dog Excellent") to his name.

Thanks, Spot, for being my partner and friend during the past twelve-plus years. Yes, now I'll stop typing and throw the toy for you again.

KATHY GRINER

Chloe Moros ("Chloe")

I became part of the Moros clan Christmas Eve 2000. It was a big surprise to my mom, and from what she tells me, the best gift she ever got. With a big red bow on my head, I pranced over to my mama and it was love at first sight. Although I am very tiny and weigh only two pounds, I am very worldly. In fact, the day after I was given to my mom, I flew to Washington, D.C., and I didn't get scared or cry even once. Since then I have flown over a dozen times. I even got to sit in the cockpit with the pilot once, which was very exciting. The pilot said all he needed was some salt and pepper and I could be his lunch. I didn't find that very funny though; neither did my mom.

After that first flight to Washington, my mom and I were getting along famously. After only a week together, I did scare her to death one night. I had a hypoglycemic attack. My mom cried and cried and took me to the emergency room. I have to admit, I was pretty scared too. I weighed only eleven ounces, and I got real sick. My mom and the vet took very good care of me, and I soon got better. Since then I have had lot's of fun. I have a best friend named Cody, another Chihuahua that I play with all the time. He lives with my grandma, grandpa, and my Uncle Bryan. Although he's bigger than me, I'm still older than he is so I boss him around a lot. We always fight for who gets to lay in the bed.

My mom says that I am very smart, which I agree with. I can sit, shake hands, and I even do this really neat trick called "Super Dog"—my mom holds me high up in the air and I stick my front paws together out in front of me and pretend that I'm flying. I make everyone laugh and giggle when I do that. My proudest moment though was when I walked in the Southbridge Pet Parade. I wore a pretty pink dress, and Mom painted my nails and put a beautiful necklace on me. Although I decided to be stubborn and not do any tricks, I won a *huge* trophy for being the "Cutest Pet." My mom very proudly displays my trophy next to my picture at home. I am a very happy girl; and as my mom says, I'm the cutest Chihuahua that ever lived. I think that I agree with her.

CHLOE

CHASE CANTEY SPROTT
("CHASE")

Woof! I am a wire-haired fox terrier, who as a young pup moved to a grand house in the Historic District. Since then my life has been full of adventures. My first day home I got to explore a much bigger world than I was used to. And I learned I could not walk on water (stupid koi pond).

After that I got to start meeting new people. I love dogs, but I like people even better. I think that because of my personality and disposition I have made many friends. I go to work with my daddy every day, and all the ladies there love me. They say I am the best doorbell that they ever had. Sometimes I come home with lipstick on top of my head from all the kisses.

We also have a country place with woods and a lake, where I have spent many hours swimming, scaring fish and birds, and chasing small animals. A few years ago we got a new neighbor, a beautiful blue shelty named Harry Barker [see *Savannah Dogs*, pages 205–6]. I fell in love, but our affaire wasn't secret for long as we were seen frequently romping in Chippewa Square and the DAR Cemetery.

Since I was asked to model for the Harry Barker

catalog, my wardrobe has become quite extensive. I love being in front of the camera. It makes me feel so glamorous. They say I am a "one shot" model. I even got a fan letter from a lady in California. And I got an offer to go to New York to try out for some commercials, but since I had just had my eleventh birthday and was not able to stand on my feet all day, I had to turn them down.

A year ago a new friend, P. J., a Jack Russell terror —I mean terrier—moved in with us. Now my time is spent keeping my people happy and teaching P. J. to respect me. He is learning that I am the boss. He will also be learning how to share toys and treats, how to avoid getting yelled at while riding in the car, and how to spot a squirrel from across the square (my specialty). Of course good behavior in the square is important because many tour carriages come by and observe our grace and Southern charm. This is a great place for a dog to live, but when people visiting Savannah talk about their dogs and how much they miss them, I realize their dogs are happy dogs too. Happiness is where you get your noogies.

CHASE

SPICE CORTESE ("SPIC")

I am a member of the Cortese family, and we all reside on Gaston Street in Savannah. I am a black Lab and was one of the very first Spice Girls. (I confess, my roots are in England.) I take a lot of teasing from my family and friends because of my name, but I always answer to it. No one can believe that I am four years old (that's twenty eight in people years), since I look and act so much younger. I am very slender and small for a Lab, weighing only fifty-five pounds, and am quite svelte. Between my figure and my abundant energy, I am often mistaken for a puppy. This might also have something to do with the fact that I am often seen carrying my "blankie" around. I don't understand why this amuses people so much. After all, I've had it since I was eight weeks old. Not only does it give me great emotional comfort, but it's also multifunctional. I can use it as a pull-toy, a pillow, and, yes, even a blanket when I'm cold. And as a proxy for a fallen bird, I can shake it nonstop! (I like to stay in touch with my inner retriever.)

In spite of my youthful appearance, I have many adult responsibilities within our family—in fact, I am entrusted with several critical duties. My first—and I must admit, favorite—job is official taster for the Cortese family. My Aunt Laura calls me a goat for my ability to eat any chewable substance. While I do prefer meats, carrots, lettuce, sushi, and salads, I have been known to eat electrical tape, plastic bags, aluminum foil, and other more challenging substances. No one seems to understand that we Labs are insatiable, and when nothing else is available, can be very creative in identifying nontraditional food items to sate our appetites. We're on permanent *see*food diets.

My second job is official greeter of any and all visitors to our household. I take this particular function very seriously and believe that *all* guests deserve a welcome more traditionally reserved for, say, masters returning from extended war duty. I kiss and hug all guests, and then I run around them. I bring them all my toys, one by one, until my toy box is empty. I flop on my back and allow them to rub my belly. I insist that they scratch my ears. I follow them around; and if they let down their guard for even a second, I sit on their laps. Everyone feels most welcomed from this treatment.

My final job is backup security guard. Dune [see *Savannah Dogs*, pages 103–5], my stepbrother, a scrawny yellow Lab mix, maintains the first line of security for our household. He's always on guard and can be counted on to hear the faintest of intrusions onto our property. If you ask me, I think he sometimes just gets bored and entertains himself by pretending that our security has been breached, but I'll never tell. I'm right there, ready to join in the "alarm system," barking and scampering madly between all the doors. This is even more fun at 2:00 or 3:00 in the morning and is sure to spur a family activity with everyone waking up and running around checking for intruders. We are guaranteed a treat for performing our jobs so vigilantly. Dune and I particularly like to tease the horses of the tour carriages that pass our house—oops, I mean protect our home from the tour carriages. We wait for the light to turn green on Whitaker Street, and begin to bark and follow them as they pass in front of our house. It took us a long time to realize that they weren't giant dogs; but by the time we figured this out, we had already developed this security exercise to a fine art. Me, I think the tourists like this homey touch of seeing how we real Savannahians live.

SPICE

SEBASTIAN MARTIN

Sebastian is a thirteen-year-old, black-and-white Shih Tzu. He was lost and alone near Isle of Hope when I found him in December 1993. Basically skin, bones, and matted hair, he was a far cry from the handsome little fellow he is today. After a trip to the vet for several flea baths, shots, worming, and neutering, it was determined that he was approximately five years old. When Sebastian first came home, he was very cautious, distrustful, and nervous. He was also anemic from the fleas and ticks. Particularly snappy with men, he would often nip at their heels or calves when they would go to leave, as if hurrying them along.

With much love and patience over a two-year period, Sebastian really blossomed, and is a testimony to what love can do. Sebastian is now the head of the Martin household.

Sebastian loves his toys, and every evening when I get home from work he brings his toy teddy bear for a daily tug of war. If he doesn't get the attention he expects, he will bark and continue to pursue the attention until he gets it. Sebastian loves to go for walks in Hull Park, which is the nearest open space to his midtown home. The round-trip walk is sometimes too much for the little fellow, but I'll gladly carry him the last block. Sometimes we think Sebastian just wants to show who is boss. Very protective of his home, Sebastian checks out all new visitors very carefully. Once he is satisfied that they mean no harm, he welcomes them.

Sebastian's late-evening routine is a favorite of mine. He jumps on the bed and lies on my chest. He wraps his paws around my neck and hugs me while showering my chin with kisses. Once this nightly routine is finished, Sebastian is satisfied that his world is secure and curls up on the foot of the bed to sleep.

Sebastian is a true hero. One day, while my mother was going through chemotherapy, Sebastian began running back and forth from the kitchen to the adjoining study barking loudly. This alerted my mother to the fact that there was a fire on the stove. A few more minutes and there would have been a disaster. Sebastian was rewarded with a juicy steak for dinner.

Sebastian is a true little buddy to me, and the love and companionship he gives has helped through difficult losses of family members and friends. The only reminder of Sebastian's unknown past is how nervous and unhappy he gets when he is left alone. Happily, someone always comes home to Sebastian these days.

Everyone who has witnessed the miraculous transformation from skinny, scared, nervous little dog, to a confident, lovable, full-of-spirit fur ball is amazed. Sebastian is truly a testimony to love and to the special bond that can develop between a dog and his companion. Of course that bond goes both ways.

KARL MARTIN

PENAPOLI
("BUBBY")

I'm a Shar-Pei–Lab mix. I was rescued from the Humane Society when I was just a few weeks old. I had a wrinkly face when I was a pup, but I've grown into my baby fat now that I'm a year old. My coat is shiny black with traces of brown, and I have a long white stripe that runs down my chest. I'm a sassy dog. I used to get into a lot of trouble when I was home alone—got into the cabinets, chewed up cereal boxes, shredded magazines that were lying around. Now I just lie on my plush dog bed and relax until Lindsay, my owner, gets home. My mommy calls me "wiggle butt" because when she gets home I get so excited that my wagging tail makes my whole butt wiggle.

Everyone is always telling me how pretty I am. I have been in two movies so far seeing as how Lindsay is a film-video major in college. My big screen debut was in the film *Samson*. Besides acting, my other activities include pulling my mommy around the park while she rides her skateboard. Since she can't keep up with me when running, it is a good workout because I can run as fast as I want while she rides the skateboard. Then, if there are no cops around, I get let off my leash so that I can chase squirrels. I haven't caught one yet, but I've come close. Sticks are another fun part about the park. I'm not too good at fetch though. I'd rather eat the stick than chase after it.

On my free time I play with my friends Linus and Ozzy, and sometimes I get to see my boyfriend, Buddy. Buddy is naughty and doesn't listen well to his owner, but I like crazy boys. I like to lie by the window and watch everyone out in the park while I chew on my toys. Every time I get a dog bone I prance around the house with it in my mouth. My mommy thinks it's really cute. Sometimes Murph lets me play with her gerbils, but when I start to lick my lips she takes them away. She thinks I want to eat those nasty rodents, but I wouldn't. Roaches are fun to play with too. I paw them until they stop moving, and then my owner has to clean them up.

I hate getting baths and I don't like to swim, so you could say I'm not a water dog. Besides those two things, I'm down for anything. I'm a social dog, and I'm well behaved, so I get to tag along with my mommy all the time. You can find me at Forsyth Park any day of the week, and I hope that we will get to meet sometime soon.

PENAPOLI

PENAPOLI

CASSIDY ROSENGART

I can't see as well as I used to; they tell me that I have cataracts. I can't hear as well I used to; it's those low tones that pass me by. I can't walk as well as I used to; it's my hips. "Arthritis" they tell me. I do fairly well on level ground, but climbing stairs is torture. I used to race up and down the stairs like a mountain goat. But my balance, my poor vision, and my hips just won't let me do it anymore. I'm embarrassed to admit it, but I also have accidents, occasionally I dribble. They say it's more common in females, but I don't like it because I smell.

I don't really mind getting old; I'm not really complaining. My appetite is good and I eat well. There's just one thing that bothers me. I think a lot about the past fifteen years. I never really got to know my mother very well, and I didn't know my father at all. My mother was a socialite, a high-class, full-blooded collie. No one will talk about my dad. I've heard in whispers that Mama was date-raped at school by a German shepherd or a golden retriever. It must have been very difficult for my mother because Dad didn't stick around and Mom tried to raise me alone. But it must have been too

28

hard. Maybe that is why I was adopted by this new family. I'm not angry with my mother. I understand.

My new family has been wonderful, especially Vanessa. I have never understood why she named me "Cassidy." That's a boy's name. She said she got the name from Hopalong Cassidy. Maybe it was because I was hyperactive when I was young. I may have had an attention deficit disorder, but they never put me on Ritalin so I don't know. Carl used to get impatient with me. Elaine was a nurse on psychiatry, so maybe she understood that I couldn't help it.

I love them deeply and dearly; I may be too attached to them. I get very anxious whenever they go away. I'm always afraid that they will never come back like my biological mother. Even though none of them looks anything like me, they are my family. They feed me, they hug and kiss me, they take me to the doctor, they brush my hair, they play with me, and they teach me so much.

For all of that I am very grateful. There isn't anything in the world I wouldn't do for them. Oh, yes, the one thing that bothers me: I'm a little bit sorry that I cannot do as much for them as I could when I was younger. My eyelashes have turned white, and I'm not as sleek as I was. But no matter how much my hips hurt, I will always stand up and hobble over to greet them. I'll wag my tail and smile. And whenever someone comes near our house, even though I can't see or hear too well, I will bark and protect them. I still can smell. That's the least I can do. And as long as I can do it . . . I will.

CASSIDY

29

VINCENT II
("VINNY")

Girls in green-and-blue plaid skirts brushed past, giving me little pats as they scrambled toward their lockers. It was 8:00 in the morning, and my day was just beginning. I heaved an exasperated sigh and collapsed on the floor, anxiously awaiting a free period or study hall. I attend St. Vincent's Academy and serve as the mascot. I am loved and adored by more than four hundred girls, and am probably the luckiest dog alive. My name is Vincent II. I am a two-year-old golden retriever and spend seven hours a day in the counselor's office at S.V.A. I proudly wear a tag stating, "I am a therapy dog," a title I received from Therapy Dogs International, after several months of training.

You may wonder why my name ends with Roman numeral II (denoting that another dog came before me). It is true. There was a Vincent I, who once was the beloved mascot for St. Vincent's Academy. He succumbed to bone cancer a month before his fourth birthday. The senior class of 2000 and the soccer team gave money toward the purchase of a new mascot out of their love for Vincent I. So, you can see, I had some big paws to fill. Everyone tells me, however, that I am a great mascot, including the Sisters of Mercy (the administrators of S.V.A.), so I feel quite secure.

My day consists of waking Jody, my mom, at 5:00 in the morning to take a walk, making sure Chelsea and Zach, my sister and brother, head safely off to school, and then hopping in the car and driving with my mom, the guidance counselor of S.V.A., to school. From there, I relax in the office, greet a few students, and munch on my breakfast. During free periods and study halls, girls grab my leash, and we walk through the cemetery, where I chase squirrels so they won't disturb the dead. Some days are more difficult than others at school. Sometimes I am required to use all my therapy skills to help girls having a rough day. Tearfully they tell me the problems that they are having with other friends or academics. I try to console them, and my mom offers suggestions to remedy the problems. When school is over, Mom and I rush home so we can take the kids to their extracurricular activities.

My cat is always waiting at the door for me when I get home from my day at school. We often play a rousing game of "bat the ball" as we wait for the kids. Zach gets home first, says "hello" to Mom, gives me a pat, and charges up the stairs to play video games. Chelsea comes home a little later, slams her heavy book bag on the floor, gives Mom a hug, and does the thing most important to her survival—gives me attention. She scratches me behind the ears, tells me about her day (which sounds extremely boring, might I add), and picks up the cat. I often get jealous when she tries to snuggle with the cat, so, of course, I try to get in her lap. She usually screams when I do this. I don't know why, but Mom says she does it because I am heavier than she is.

Later we take Chelsea and Zach to all their extra-curricular activities, including ballet, soccer, and piano, and eat dinner. Dad comes home around 7:00, pats my back, and helps the kids with their homework. Dad takes me on a walk around midnight. Then I hop under the covers with whichever family member allows me and fall into a deep sleep. Yes, this is just a day in the life of Vincent II, mascot at St. Vincent's Academy and loving member of the Riddle household.

VINNY

CAPTAIN RHETT'S BABY FOOTS ("FOOTS")

Oh, I've heard them all: "Did'ja get a saddle with that dog?" "Is that a seeing-eye dog?" "Who's walkin' who there?"

I don't think they were trying to be mean—I'm just a great big dog. I seem to be much bigger than most dogs I come across. And sometimes they give me that look, like, "You're not so big." But I am. I'm just a great big dog. A Great Dane, or so I'm told.

I've lived in Savannah my whole life, and they say I've lived a very charmed life. I met my mama when I was six weeks old, and we went to work right away. As a matter of fact, I went to work with Mama every day. She worked where people get pictures made near the post office downtown. It was great to sit in the window and watch all of Savannah go by. Sometimes Savannah would come in to see me. If they were getting their pictures, they would always speak to me or pat my head. Even out-of-towners would stop and visit. Some regulars would bring me treats. Some would be very surprised, even scared, to see me. Go figure.

I could always count on the Girl Scouts, who were

just around the corner, to come by and see me from time to time, maybe share a cookie with me, even though my favorite food is french fries. (But don't tell Mama.) I love kids and even helped raise a few, from just a few weeks old to some grown-ups that acted just like kids.

One man would see me through the glass and get down on his hands and knees and try to talk to me in my own language. That was fun. That same man was working for a company that made trucks or something, and that had the same name as me. One night he took me to River Street for an important meeting that his company was having. You should have seen me walk into that hotel with all those people in their good clothes. I held my head high as they all pointed and said, "Look at that Great Dane." No other dogs were invited. Ever since then I knew I was special.

Once I was asked to be in a commercial for a car. All the cameras and lights were really exciting. But, you know, I never saw a car the whole time. All they asked me to do was walk across the street with a pretty girl. That was it. And I never saw the commercial.

I met a lot of people during the big parades every year, even though I stayed behind the glass the whole time. Everyone who knew me asked about me, and those who didn't know me wanted to.

All of that glitz and glamour, however, just isn't for me. I enjoy just being with my friends and family, especially Mama. Even though I pull her around by the leash and try to go where I want to go, we have a good time. She loves me and I wouldn't change a thing.

FOOTS

KAJAH MARRAH ("KAJAH-ROO," "ROOFUS")

I am a gorgeous—at least that's what my mommy tells me—weimaraner. My mommy and I live on Jones Street. We are originally from Michigan, and we moved here so that she can go to school at SCAD and someday be a great interior designer. Although I hate it when she has to go to class, she makes it up to me by taking me to the park to play with all my friends. My very best friends are Winston and Wylly [see *Savannah Dogs*, pages 241–44]. They live downstairs and are the coolest. They have taught me the ropes around here, and we could play together for hours.

When Mommy and I get home from the park, we have dinner and then Mommy does her homework. I am a big help when it comes to homework. I'm responsible for the comic relief so that she doesn't get stressed out. When she starts to get too serious, I tell her how much I love her by giving her lots of kisses, and I even try to give her my toys to play with. That usually makes her feel better.

Our favorite part of the week is the weekend because that's when we really cut loose. Mommy and I go everywhere together, and she always rolls down the car window so that I can pretend that I'm flying. I love it when Mommy turns up the music at home and we cut a rug together. I'm an excellent dancer. The very best weekends are when Daddy visits. He goes to school in Jacksonville. I really miss him when he's away. When we're together, I am so happy because I have the best family in the world. I love them very much.

It's really great living here in Savannah. Everyone is so nice, and they watch out for Mommy and me. It's like one big family. There are so many cool dogs living on my block—Dune [see *Savannah Dogs*, pages 228–33], Bella, and Hatcher, just to name a few. We all keep the neighborhood safe by always keeping an eye out for trouble. Although I'm still just a little pup, I've had the best life, and it's all because of the wonderful people I've met along the way. I'm so happy that I grew up in Savannah, with its beautiful squares, warm weather, kind people, and great trees for the hunting of squirrels.

KAJAH

TOBY BRUNSWICK, JR. ("TOBY," "TOBS," "MR. TOOBS")

I've been to Wal-Mart enough times to know about the fairly friendly sole who welcomes you into Walton's world and makes you feel nice. I think that their position is known as the "Wal-Mart Greeter," and their job is to smile and make you feel that the store is better than K-Mart.

I did not feel welcome tonight. When I entered, the lady sucked her teeth and looked the other way. There were no huggies. I looked around for that warm face and that not-just-country, but that country-country, accent by my Wal-Mart Greeter. They had plucked them all up for those Supercenter commercials.

When I got to the door of my home, I could hear "the boy" growling and jumping to the sound of my keys. "I'm glad you're back. Here's a shoe," he sang and wiggled. I smiled. Toby had done it again.

If you closed your eyes while Toby greeted me, you might be thinking "Cujo," but if you've known Toby all his seven years you'd believe me when I say that the boy put the golden in retriever.

Born with show-dog blood in him, he had his path mapped out. There was a wrinkle, however, that crept

37

down Toby's nose that would end a silly show-dog career that was never meant to be.

"It would be a waste not to show him," said the lady whom we had gotten him from. Yea, right.

She continued with something ridiculous. "They have people who can disguise his wrinkle before the show." Did someone say Botox?

Since we had trophies, we decided we wanted just a dog.

Done with his serenading, Tobs looked up at me. "Something the matter?"

I replied, "Went to Wal-Mart and the greeter sucked her teeth at me."

He curled up in a ball, not letting a single hair hang beyond the fringe of the small island of a rug he was on, and then he gave his golden advice: "Well, I'm sure it wasn't just you she did it to."

"You're absolutely right. She did it to the folks in front of me. They always make those greeters look so nice on TV, don't they? I wonder if they really did use up all the good ones for the Supercenter commercials. Maybe she was just having a bad day."

Always giving people a chance, Toby proposed that maybe the greeter didn't have a dog at home to love and take care of.

"Hey! I know, Toby. The way you greeted me was fantastic. You always make our family feel better with your singing and wiggling. Why don't you be a Wal-Mart Greeter? Everyone would just love you. It would be Rollback Utopia, and they have lots of shoes."

"Hey, Toby, I know you're about to go on break, so if you're hungry you can have my leftover ham sand-wich in the break room. I usually bring it home for my

38

dog, but since it's your first day and all . . . and, hey, could you grab me a toothpick when you're done. It's insane how I get this ham stuck in my teeth all the time. Thanks."

LESLIE MOSES

LADY
("LADY-LOU," "LEWSKY")

Lady became part of my family against my wishes. After all, we already had a dog, Toby, a male golden retriever [see pages 37–39], and a cat. My husband saw a dog crossing White Bluff Road during busy afternoon traffic. He stopped and tried to get her in the car, but she refused. He tied his tie around her neck and walked her all the way to our house. We saw that she was a red golden retriever, and surely someone was missing her. We placed an ad in the paper with no results. My family thought we should keep her. I thought otherwise. She dug tunnels in our yard, and she barked at every neighbor who dared to venture out into their yard. I, however, was outnumbered in my opinion of her.

My husband named her and took her to the vet for shots. The vet said he couldn't tell if she was "fixed," but that we would soon know. We did. She wasn't. Lady was a fast runner who loved to chase tennis balls. We noticed that she was moving a bit slower, and her middle moved from side to side when she ran. Soon there was no doubt that she was pregnant. Our two gol-

40

dens were going to have puppies. The vet examined her and said he felt six puppies in her belly.

I still was not completely sold on Lady. When she had her first puppy, she sniffed him, growled at him, and ran away. Finally, after having more puppies, she nursed him with the rest. When she finished, she had delivered twelve puppies.

I had reservations about Lady's ability "to mother." She only had eight breasts, so some puppies missed feedings because they couldn't "get to the table." We decided to help her. We would rotate puppies at feeding time so that they could all get a turn to eat. Lady was very hungry all the time after she had had her puppies. If she smelled food cooking in the kitchen and was feeding her puppies, she would stand up with eight pups attached to her breasts and drop them, then run into the kitchen to get something to eat. What kind of mother is that? I wondered. We took turns bribing Lady with large bowls of puppy food. We would hold the bowls up to her to eat out of while she nursed her puppies.

My daughter, Leslie, came home one night from her job upset about something at work. As she lay on the bed telling me her tale of woe, Lady stood and watched. She had eight mammary glands full of milk. As Leslie began to cry, Lady jumped up on top of her, smothering her with her breasts, and began licking her tears away. Immediately the tears were replaced with laughs. That was when my heart completely melted for Lady. I realized that I had helped Lady mother her babies and she had helped me mother mine.

Lady has been a part of my family and my heart for over six years now, and I can't imagine life without her.

LYNN MOSES

41

EMPRESS
SAMANTHA
("SAMMIE," "SAM")

I was born in Connecticut, and was chosen by my owner, Barbara, because of my beautiful face. When I was taken to the vet for my first examination, Barbara was told, "You're going to have trouble with this one. She's definitely an alpha dog, and likes her own way." I was only eight weeks old. Truer words were never spoken.

Easy to housebreak, other aspects of puppy training did not go so well. From day one I hated being kenneled. After one night of howling, Barbara thought it would be fun to have me sleep with her in bed at her feet. Husband Bud wasn't keen on the idea, but another sleepless night was out of the question, so why not? I was much happier, being with my new human "pack," but demanded to sleep above them, taking my place on the shelf behind the pillows. This worked well until I started growing, and at about fifty pounds I was getting too big for the shelf. So I moved myself down to the pillows, insisting that I be above the others in my pack. Barbara and Bud were forced to accommodate me, taking new, very interesting sleeping positions.

During puppyhood I was taken to the dog park for daily exercise and socialization with other puppies.

Most of the time I preferred to sit to one side, just watching the others, rarely "mixing it up" with them. I've always been "laid back." Once, there were about ten Labrador puppies in the park at the same time, all playing together, except me, who was just sitting and watching. Barbara asked the other owners how old their puppies were, and received answers like "Mine's six months," "Mine's ten," "Mine's seven and a half." When one owner asked Barbara how old Sammie was, she said, "Mine's ten." The surprised woman said, "Wow, she's in great shape for a ten-*year*-old dog."

My owners tried to teach me games, but that seemed so stupid. One game was to throw this ball. Why should I go get it, when they threw it? I just would sit there and watch them. Finally they would have to get it. Then they'd throw it again, so I'd sit there until they went to get it again. What a waste of energy.

As a puppy, I loved the smell of shoes. Whenever I found one, my owners would get very excited and make lots of noise, so I would try and go to a quiet place with my new "treasure." Well, they'd follow me and try to take it away, but I was very quick. Finally Barbara taught me the word "trade"—if I would give her the shoe, she would give me a cookie. What a great game. Now, whenever I want a cookie, I just look for a shoe, or any other treasure I shouldn't have, and I get a treat. Works every time.

I was very happy with my pack, especially in the winter. I loved the cold weather and snow; the deeper, the better. I also loved rides in the car, always insisting on riding shotgun. Things were quite under control until I took a very long ride to a very strange place where it was hot. There were lots of bugs and lots of water that I couldn't swim in. Then all the furniture from my old home arrived, and I realized that this would be my new home. For a long time I missed my buddies and my dog park, but Barbara tried to make it fun for me, finding new places to swim and meet new friends. It took a while, but I finally got used to a different way of life here.

After living here a few months, I met a new friend, MacSie, a German shorthaired pointer. Although she was just a baby when I met her, we've become good friends. She has way too much energy, but we get along great; and when she gets too wild, I just put my paw on her and smack her down. Sometimes we have "sleep-overs." When our families are away and we have to board out, we get to stay together, so we can get into trouble together.

When I'm home alone with Barbara and Bud, we have playtime after dinner. Bud sits in his easy chair to watch TV. I bring him my favorite ball, place it at his feet, and make noise until he throws it. He has to throw the ball down the hall. I'll bring it back and give it to him, as long as I get a cookie as a reward. We do this five or six times, until I'm full. By the way, this is the only time I'll chase a ball. Outdoors, it's just too much effort, and I can get treats other ways, like stealing things I shouldn't have . . . *trade*.

I still miss the snow and cold weather. It gets so hot here that I sometimes refuse to go for my walk. I'll go to the end of the driveway; and if I feel the heat and humidity, I'll just sit down and refuse to go any farther. I've finally trained both Barbara and Bud to pay attention to me. For fun they'll take me for rides in the golf cart. I like that because I don't have to exert too much energy. If the weather is cool, we go on some great adventures in the woods and marshes. I've met some very interesting animals here, like crabs, snakes, alligators, and deer. I think they scare Barbara more than me. All in all, I love my life here in Savannah.

EMPRESS SAMANTHA

TRIXEE-DOG DOSER ("TRIXEE," "TRIXSTER," "TRIX")

Woof! Arf-arf! I'm also known as Trixee-Lixee the Kissy Dog because I live to lick and love. (Just get your face close enough and I'll show ya! Doggie kisses heal whatever ails you.) Daddy says I'm his little buddy, and Mommy says I'm the coolest dog on the planet. I am part dachshund, part spaniel, and part speculation. Mommy and Daddy adopted me from Save-A-Life when I was just four months old, and soon I'll be six years old.

From my tail-wagging, wake-up thump-thump-thump at 5:00 A.M. until bedtime, I have so much to do every day. Eating, napping, playing, chasing the cat, romping, and barking at the neighbors—I am a very busy doggie.

I am a total indoor doggie, but I like to play outside too. I play Olympic Doggie—I run around the yard in a figure eight as fast as I can. (I always win the gold biscuit.) I like to chase the neighborhood ducks, but Mommy keeps me on a leash—it's for my own good, blah-blah-blah . . . whatever—so I can't get too close to the quackers. When Mommy is outside, I want to be outside too. But Savannah summers are so hot, and I like to be inside because I'm an air-conditioned doggie. Besides, too much heat makes my hair frizzy.

I have my own cat. She is pretty cool for a cat, but I like my toy basket better. I like to play fetch and tug. I can dance too. I swing my little body from left to right and then howl like a wolf. That's called "the Trixee dance." Sometimes I get so excited that my daddy says I vibrate.

Mommy spoils me, and Daddy is the discipliner. He yells "No!" and calls me "bad girl" when I do something bad, but then Mommy pets me, gives me a treat, and calls me "good girl." I can do tricks too, so if I really want a biscuit, I sit up and beg. (I taught myself that one.) Or if I want my favorite, a hiney-scratch or belly-rub, I will lie down at your feet and roll and wiggle around on the floor until I get one.

Mommy says that I am a mischievous puppy. When Mommy and Daddy are busy working in the yard and aren't watching me too close, I roll around in the ducky poop. Of course Daddy then has to give me a bath, and I hate bath time. But I love rolling in ducky poop. I usually get a bath after I've had a haircut. After bathtime I run around the house at full canine speed until I'm so tired I just flop down and take a nap.

Do you like my picture? I'm a real rockin' dog. Mommy thinks I'm the cutest thing on four paws. It's totally groovy to be coolest dog on the planet. And now I'm a celebrity too. After all, I am famous enough to be in *Savannah Dogs*. Here's barkin' at'cha.

TRIXEE

47

LACEY MIKELL

I am an Australian shepherd, and I am amazing—at least my mom is always telling me so. I don't exactly hear her, but a dog can sense these things. You see I was born blind and deaf. People kept telling my mom that it would be better if I was put to sleep, but she just wanted to give me the best life I could have. My mom thought that I would only survive about six months. She bought a dog kennel for me and thought that I would have to spend my time outside in it. I love to be outside and not cooped up in the house. I don't know what the big deal is about not being able to see or hear, but then again I never did see or hear. I didn't stay in that kennel but for a day. When I was outside, I would hold on to my momma dog's ear to get around. It did not take long for me to know every inch of the property. When I wake up from a nap, I give a quick spin and I always know exactly where I am.

When I was six months old, a pig got in our yard. I didn't know what a pig was, but it smelled awful. I was terified and ran to get away. When my mom drove home that day, the other dogs were waiting in the road to be rescued, but I had gotten lost. The temperature got below freezing that night. For three days, day and night, my family looked for me in the fields and woods around our house. They put posters all around our neighborhood, but no one had seen me. My family thought they had lost me forever. Being able to see and hear didn't help them find me. I had to use my sense of smell and touch to find my own way home. When I arrived home after three days without so much as a scratch, my mom cried and my family kept telling me what an amazing dog I was.

It has been eight years since I got lost. I never go out of the yard now, unless it is to go for a walk with my mom or dad. I like to chase the squirrels, and I can stop just short of running into the tree. None of my dog family is able to sneak and get any of my food; I know where they are at all times. I am always the first to walk down the drive to greet family and friends; and so that they don't get lost, I lead them back to the house. Those people now think I live a very good life. Did I tell you that my mom thought I was amazing?

LACEY

TOO CUTE
OSCAR BARNEY
FORD
("T. C.")

I was born in May 1997. As soon as my eyes opened, I knew the world was my oyster.

My dad mostly calls me T-Man or Mister T. He's the one who succumbed to my charms first. While my mom was holding my brother and admiring him, I knew I quickly had to do something. So I attacked my mom's shoelaces, and that got my dad's attention. He was hooked, and the rest is history.

At first, for about two nights, I slept in a room by myself, then my dad brought me into the bed with them, which made me happy. Sometimes my parents complain because I like to sleep crosswise in the bed and crowd them to the very edge. Hey, I don't like to be crowded, so this keeps them off of me.

My mom calls me lots of embarrassing names, such as Pootuie, Pumpkin, Sugar Plum, Sweet Cakes, and her Little Boy. She means well and I love her too, so whatever makes her happy.

I'm also called "the destroyer" because I go for the jugular of every new toy that I get. First, I immediately go for the squeaker, then I rip out the stuffing, then work on what's left. My mom good naturedly fusses about the mess I make.

If both of my parents go away at the same time, when they come home I follow them around howling and barking, letting them know I am upset at them for leaving me. They laugh at me, but I'm serious.

My mom walks for exercise, and sometimes she'll insist that I go because my girth has spread a little. But I have my conditions on that, too. My dad has to drive Mom and me a mile or so down the road, and we walk home. I refuse to leave home walking. If Mom tries to force me, I fall down, roll over on my back with my legs in the air, and refuse to budge. She's tried fussing at me and begging me to get up, but I will not. A man has to stick to his guns when principles are at stake. My parents call me a hardheaded dachshund, but I don't mind, as long as I win.

My dad tells me that I'm tough, and when he speaks to me in a certain voice, I howl. I'm a good howler, and loud.

We have two big dogs in our yard. They're supposed to guard the house and yard to keep unwanted visitors away. But most of the time they need my help. They bark, but I'm ferocious and everyone knows it. We have a huge fenced-in yard, so I have a lot of work to do.

Excuse me, but I've gotta run. I think I hear someone at the gate. Maybe it's the UPS man. I love that truck. I can hear it a long way before it gets here, and I'm outside waiting to pounce.

T. C.

MID-SUMMER NIGHT'S DREAM ("SUMMER")

That's what I was, a summer's dream, when my mom brought me home, mid-summer, July 2000. I was already four months old, but I was still very much a puppy. I lived with my furry parents during that short time. I quickly warmed up to my new mom. I was told that I was brought home to help my mom with her stress. I do such a good job. I sleep under the covers at night, snuggling right up next to her. I try to make her feel good by always being there, underfoot. I just like keeping her in sight for my own peace of mind.

I am two years old now, and I still have accidents in the house. My mother learned that Yorkshire terriers are one of the hardest breeds of puppy to potty train. I don't think this helps with her stress, but she can't stay upset with me for long. I am just too cute. I just don't like for her to leave me here while she goes to those places called "work," the Island Veterinary Clinic, or "school," the Savannah College of Art and Design. I try to tell her that I can go, but she doesn't think I would be able to stay still for that long. Maybe she is right. I do get to travel with her to Atlanta to see our family. My granny loves me to death. She thinks that I am so cute! My Uncle Brensen is my favorite. Grandpa and Grandma Danielle like their cat better, but I love them anyways. I have driven and flown numerous times back and forth from Savannah to Atlanta, and even have flown from Colorado to Atlanta after a long cross-country trip from Savannah. I am well associated with the proper etiquette of automobile and air travel. I have my own cozy bag that I ride in. I am so lucky that I am still allowed to fly, even with the more secure airline policies.

We live on Tybee Island. I love to go on walks. I am only four-and-a-half pounds, but I pull my mom during the whole time when we walk. I try to stay on the pavement because I hate the sandspurs. Ouch! I love to run on the beach, but my mom doesn't take me out there much. She says that some people just don't like sharing. She risks it sometimes because she knows how much I love it. I just can't imagine someone not sharing something so big with me being so small. Maybe one day I will be allowed on the sandy beaches. I too like the feel of the sand between my toes, the wind in my hair. At least I have a great view of the beach from my home. I still get to bark at all of those people who can walk on the beach as they walk down the catwalk. What is up with that—"cat" walk? Anyway, I love Savannah and can't imagine living anywhere else.

SUMMER

53

LADY GRACE
OF PIEDMONT
("GRACIE")

As you can see, I am the most unusual but adorable dog you have ever laid your eyes on. Yes, folks, I am a corgi.

My mom searched for six months and then found me in Piedmont, Alabama. She chose me from pictures with this thing called "E-mail." Sounds pretty weird to me. My mom and dad picked me up on the way to a racetrack in Birmingham.

It's a good thing that I'm not bashful, because I meet lots of people every day. You see, my mom works for a veterinarian. So I am like those nice people at Wal-Mart. I get to greet people, lick children, and bark at strangers all day. I also supervise the kennel. I make sure that all the boarders are behaving as they should while their parents are out of town.

After a hard day at work, with my mommy saving other pets' lives, we like to come home and relax. So she thinks. She might attempt to relax while I push my toy into her lap until she finally throws it across the room so I can attack and tear it to shreds. I have this obsession with this thing that squeaks. I just can't stand it. It drives me crazy, and I can't stop until I have ripped it from the stuffing and destroyed it. Can you believe that my mom keeps bringing me these things? As soon as she pulls them out of the bag, all I can think is, "Conquer and destroy."

After it gets dark outside, my daddy comes home and we have so much fun. I sit on the top of the couch by the picture window and watch for his truck to come down the drive. He calls for me as soon as he steps in the door. He likes for me to hang on his pants leg. Then he runs around the bar chasing me—as if I am scared. Yeah, right. Then I get to chase him. Just because I am short doesn't mean you can pick on the little dog. I may not be able to bite your hand, but I will bite whatever is closest.

On the weekend my dad plays with this thing that goes around in a circle really, really fast. They call it a racecar and it's very loud. It's not my favorite hobby, because I have big ears, you see. My mom and I get to watch from way up high in the stands. Sometimes Mom squeezes me really hard and closes her eyes. I still haven't figured out why, but everybody screams around us at the same time. It's very dramatic. Trust me, I know these things.

I have a lot of people in my life who care about me. Not only do I have my mom and dad, but I have wonderful grandparents as well. What would they all do without me? As you can see, I am a very important dog with a very hard commitment to fulfill. I have to protect my family and provide them with loyalty, love, and understanding. I am so loved.

GRACIE

CHAUNCEY HOSKING

Hello, my name is Chauncey. I am mostly Old English sheepdog and I am four years old. My story begins when I was four months old and a nice man named Lee Freeland found me running down Eisenhower in Savannah. Lee rescued me and took good care of me until Celia and her daughter Sherrill adopted me. I am the luckiest dog in town. Celia and Sherrill gave me a great home and lots of love, and spoiled me rotten.

Because I live at The Landings, I became very interested in golf. Most of the golfers at The Landings know me because I love to watch them play. They ask me which club they should use and of course tell me how cute I am. I am real good at finding golf balls. Sometimes I give them back to their owner, but most of the time I bring them home to my humans. My humans have a basket full of golf balls that I have found. I also love to ride in my golf cart.

My humans must think I am really dumb. They spell words in front of me, like c-h-e-e-s-e, and c-a-r, and s-h-o-p-p-i-n-g, and r-i-d-e. I know exactly what they are saying, but I play their silly game. I love to go to PETsMART. I know which aisle the squeaky toys are in. I dig through them until I find the one I want, and then I carry it to the register. I know Sherrill will buy me another one even though I have enough toys for a hundred dogs in my toy box at home. I love to go for rides in the car or in my golf cart. Sherrill takes me for lots of rides, but I like Celia's car the best. It has this really neat thing called a sunroof that I stick my head out of. For some reason, people give me some strange looks and point at me.

I am a social butterfly and I love to play. I might weigh ninety-five pounds, but I am very gentle with children and I have a dog friend that weighs three pounds. Everyone in the neighborhood knows me, even the mailman or mail lady. I like her the best because she has biscuits. Once I jumped in her truck to get another one, and I refused to get out. She had to take Sherrill and me for a ride around the block before I got out. I know the UPS man and the Federal Express lady too. When Sherrill takes me for a walk, she lets me sit at the side of the road and watch the world go by, and people stop to admire me. Celia says we look like the village idiots. I don't think so. It is my duty to keep an eye on my neighborhood. I know what kind of cars my neighbors drive. If there is a strange car around, I must investigate. I guess you could say that I'm nosy, but it's a great way to meet people and other dogs. I get along with all fellow canines, no matter how big or small, young or old, they are.

I am also a ham and a clown. If my humans have other people over, I demand to be the center of attention. When people have finished petting me, I put on a show with my toys. I get them all out of my toy box, throw them around, and make them squeak. If this doesn't work, I drink someone's drink or take some food. That does the trick. These strangers have the nerve to come into my house and sit on my furniture. I sit and wait until they get up and then reclaim my favorite chairs. If they refuse to move, I will sit in front of them and stomp my feet. The strangers will ask Celia or Sherrill what my problem is, and they will tell them that they are in my chair. Guess what? Most of the time the strangers will move. After all, this is my house.

As you can probably tell, I am one lucky guy. Please don't insult me by calling me a dog. I consider myself to be a human, and many others will agree with me. I want to say thank you to Lee for rescuing me. He even comes to my house to see me, but my heart belongs to Celia and Sherrill. I will always give them unconditional love and add joy and happiness to their lives. And that, folks, is my story. Please feel free to bring me a toy, some food, or just a good scratch.

CHAUNCEY

GYPSY JENKINS
("GYPSY-GIRL")

Dear Minnie,

When I heard about your wonderful book, dedicated to the veterinarians and the associations that help animals in Savannah, I knew I had to tell you my story. Dr. Bink has saved my life more than once, and I was adopted from the Humane Society. Needless to say, my family and I are indebted to them forever.

When I was less than a year old, I was hit by a car out on Highway 17 and left to die. A kind lady found me and took me to Dr. Bink, who operated on me for several hours and saved my life. He said that I was "flat as a pancake" when I arrived.

I stayed at Dr. Bink's Central Animal Hospital for about a month while I healed. Heika and everybody there treated me with love and care, and they will be my friends for life. Then Heather, Dr. Bink's wife, started taking me to the Humane Society so I could find my family.

One fine day my papa walked in, and it was love at

first sight. My mom and papa have had a great time spoiling me ever since.

Minnie, I want to share with you a poem we wrote for Dr. Bink. When l was about four, I got this horrible gastrointestinal hemorrhagic syndrome and he saved me again. That's when Mom and I decided to write our story. I hope you enjoy it. Oh, and Minnie, I'd love to meet you someday. I think we would be "soul canines."

––––––––––––––––––––––

Ode to Dr. Bink

We met in the autumn of ninety-five
When you first saw me I was barely alive

A stranger found me by the highway lying
When she brought me to you I was nearly dying

You worked and worked and brought me around
The treatment you gave me was truly profound

My short life had been filled with strife
That was the first time you saved my life

I stayed with you till I got well
And everyone treated me really swell

Then Heather took me to adopt
That's how I found my mom and pop

Since then I've filled their lives with joy
Mom says I'm just like a live stuffed toy

Papa loves to take me to the park
Where I play with C. D.—we run and bark

I had to have more surgery
You removed my pin and made a hip sling for me

To heal it took a little while
You always greeted me with a kiss and a smile

Then one day I got this awful syndrome
It threatened to topple our happy kingdom

We rushed to you and you got busy
I had my family in quite a tizzy

I'm sorry I kept Richie up all night
I had to put up a mighty strong fight

I'm sure I bothered Morgan and Heather too
But then, that sweet lady is used to a zoo

Dear Dr. Bink, we just wanted to say
Devotion like yours we could never repay

What we feel for you is more than puppy love
It's something special sent from above.

Love, and (not too wet) kisses,

GYPSY JENKINS

MS. KIZY MCVICKER JENSEN ("BABY GIRL")

I asked the Lord to send me a companion—one that would be loving, faithful, and uncomplicated. I could not have imagined what the answer would be. I had been without a pet for thirty-five years and had no intention of having another. But when the bulletin board at work advertised a mixed-breed dog for a good home, I answered the ad.

When I went by to look at the little animal, a Shih Tzu–cocker spaniel mix, I knew after picking her up that there was no way I would have such a flea-infested dog in my home. But I told the lady that I would make up my mind overnight and return the next day with my answer.

I was scheduled to meet with my sister that Saturday, and I told her that I had to go back to tell the lady that I did not want her puppy. But I did stop on the way to buy some flea powder. I could not stand the thought of that little puppy continuing to scratch like she did during our first meeting. On that occasion she had looked at me, when I picked her up, with an expression of indifference.

When we got to the puppy's home, I told the lady

that I wanted to powder the little dog so that she would not be so uncomfortable. I picked up that little floppy-eared mutt, turned her over, and completely powdered her underside. As I turned her back over, she was so close to my face that I was astonished to feel an ever so slightly lick on my cheek. It was not a kiss in the true sense of the word; it was more of a Kiz. My heart leapt, and I said to her, "Come on, Ms. Kizy, you are going home with me."

During these last three years, Kizy has remained independent and also has been a little watchdog from the moment that I brought her home. During our first evening at home, when we were sitting in the big recliner watching TV, she saw the reflection of the television picture in the sliding door and went into a rousing tirade.

She could not understand when I left her at the vet's to be spayed. And I could not tell her how I cried after I left her there. But she was a healthy young lady, in spite of the fact that her mother died from heartworm just months after Kizy's birth. And Kizy continues to fare well because she loves her doctor, even when he gives her the annual shots and exams.

When I come home from work every evening, she will stick her head out of the pump house, where she has her blankets, and make sure that it is me. Then she will run to the back of the property in an attempt to let me know that she doesn't really care if I am home or not. After all, I was the one who left her.

This past December, just before Christmas, I got home at my normal time. When I got out of my car and unlocked the gate, she ran off to the back as usual. I went to the mailbox, got my mail, came back to the car, and picked up some other items to take into the house. I got inside the gate, got my mail, and started toward to the house. Suddenly she came running at me, full speed, barking long and hard. I said to her, "Honey, what is the matter with you?" She came at me harder, barking even louder. Suddenly it dawned on me. Just as I turned back to the gate, an intruder landed on the inside of the fence. I yelled quite loudly, "I know one damn somebody that better get the hell out of my yard!" And then I said, "Take him, Ms. Lizy." She hurled all twenty-two of her pounds after him. He was fortunate in that he could leap the fence so quickly. I like to think that he is still running.

At first I did not realize the cost of owning a pet nowadays—food, vet's bills, new toys. But the cost is very little when you realize the benefits of personal safety and of unconditional love that you get in return. And this year Ms. Kizy is again the owner of pet insurance so that she will not have to endure the fate of her poor mother. And as an added bonus, when I now come home each day, my little girl meets me at the gate.

KAY L. JENSEN

DAISY

Dear Minnie,

Hi! My name is Daisy and I'm the cutest beagle there is, or at least that's what my mom and dad tell me. I'm seven years old and live with my family in the country. When I go outside, I get to see rabbits and lizards, and sometimes even a turkey. I've been lucky that I've never seen a snake, though. My parents said that they're out there, but Brutus usually barks to warn us when he sees them. Brutus is my ten-year-old brother. I think he's cool. I used to have two big, older sisters—black Labs named Maggie and Marilyn—but sadly they both died last year. I sure miss them.

My dad volunteers with the Civil Air Patrol doing search-and-rescue (SAR, for short). He says that I would make an excellent SAR partner if all pilots carried jerky in their pockets. Then I could sniff them out from miles away. When he goes out on missions, I sit in my big orange chair and stare at the back door, wishing all the while that he'll come home safe. I'm not completely happy until both my parents are home with me. Then I can relax and chew on my bone.

My mom sometimes makes homemade treats for Brutus and me. She started a small business and named it the Little Daisy Cookie Company, after me of course. My job is vice-president of Quality Control. I inspect every batch, and I haven't found a bad one yet. Mom started making doggie biscuits several years ago as holiday gifts for my doggie cousins and friends, and now they can't get enough of them. Even my dad's doggie customers are asking for them. Dad's an exterminator, so he visits lots of houses each day. He always takes time to play with the doggies that live there, and when he comes home I get to smell his shoes and sniff him to see where he's been. It's like a smell-guessing game I get to play. Did he visit Harley and Sasha today? Or was it Buster and Shelby? Was it Max and Willie? Or maybe it was Maggie? There are always so many smells.

One of my favorite things to do is to go for rides in the truck. My family goes on vacation to Florida each year, and sometimes we visit my grandparents in Dublin. During the trip I have the whole backseat to myself, but sometimes I climb up front and sit between Mom and Dad. Wherever we go, people are always stopping to pet me and to tell me how cute I am. When we stay at a hotel, I like to walk up and down the stairs just for fun. Did you know that there are some hotels that don't allow doggies? I think that's just silly—after all, most of us make less of a mess than the people do.

Well, thanks for letting me share my story with you and your readers. I'll be sure to have my mom send you some homemade biscuits soon. You'll love them.

Your friend,

DAISY

ANNABELLE LEE
SATURDAY
("ANNIE")

Annie was a mid-life dog, coming at the time in my life when our last child was off to college and I had remodeled the kitchen, choosing the white floor that everyone told me not to use. I still remember my fateful words to explain my choice: "But we don't have any dogs or children at home, so it won't be a problem with just the two of us." Then our daughter decided that she wanted a dog for her birthday, and Annabelle Lee came into our lives. The plan was for Annie to live with her mistress in her apartment at school, but that didn't last long. One day a police officer rang our doorbell and asked if we had anyone from our address living in Statesboro. Since both of our children were students at Georgia Southern at the time, we were extremely relieved to find out that the officer was referring to Annie. It seems that Annie somehow got out and wandered down the street in Statesboro until she saw an open door. She let herself in and took a seat on the couch, waiting for someone to find her. Her tags gave our Savannah address, so the Statesboro police called the Savannah police and a kind officer came to inform us that Annie had been found. The problem was that when we called our daughter, she didn't know that Annie was missing. Someone visiting the apartment had accidentally let her out, and no one knew she was gone. That was when Annie began an extended stay with us. She quickly ruled the roost in our empty-nest household. She was the smartest, cutest, most agreeable, friendliest—you get the picture. The next thing I knew, we had decided to mate her so we would always have one of her offspring.

We were told a good dog would try to prove herself by having a large litter, and Annie did just that. She had twelve puppies in her first litter, but she really proved herself during the birth. When she went into labor, she produced nine puppies with no help and no fuss. Four hours later she was in a box in our kitchen with the babies when she started making some noises. We called the vet, and as we were talking he heard her. Even though it was 10:30 and he had just gotten home and hadn't eaten dinner yet, he said for us to bring her to his office immediately. He X-rayed her and found a puppy was turned sideways in the birth canal. My husband had to assist the vet with the cesarian, but we left with Annie and three more puppies to add to the ones we had at home. They all lived, even the puppy that had been stuck in the birth canal for hours. Annie nursed all twelve and we entertained visitors. Our doorbell was always ringing. A dozen golden retriever puppies are irresistible. Annie's puppy album has eleven family portraits of the puppies and their new families. The twelfth is of Annie and the puppy we kept, Scout, but that's a story for *Savannah Dogs III*.

DIANE SATURDAY

PORTIA TUCKER McLAUGHLIN ("TORTILLA")

Hi! Portia here. Before you hear my story, you need to know some things about me. First thing is, I'm a dog. More particularly, a black bassadore. A bassadore? Yup, that's what I said. Bassadores are Labradors and bassets mixed. Get it? Bassadore. I have beautiful brown eyes and shining fur, and my legs are short. I feel that long legs are a waste of muscle. Who needs it when my short legs take me everywhere I need to go? It's just a waste. Anyway, just so you know, I like to eat. And I'm not a picky eater either. Give me anything, anytime.

Ya'll are just about to hear a magnificent, a spectacular, a stupendous story . . . starring me. Okay, here goes. Once, about five years ago, I was born. I lived with a couple of people who were okay, but they sometimes forgot to feed me. Soon they moved away, leaving me at my vet's office. I was sad to see them go. The people at the vet's were really nice; they played with me, but I wanted a family. Then I was put up for adoption. Many families tried to take me home, but they either had other dogs—and I got jealous and growled—or fences that I tried to dig under. And so, people brought me back. For example, my first family had three large, mean, ugly dogs that growled at me a lot. So, of course, I growled back and got sent back to the vet's. My second family had a lovely garden. I couldn't resist digging in it, and wouldn't you know it, I was sent back. My third family had a great backyard and a large, strong fence surrounding it. One day I decided to see the world and dug underneath it. The people—well, you guessed it—sent me back.

I stayed at the vet's for three years, giving blood to dogs who needed it in surgery. Later, at Thanksgiving, when I was four, a nice man and woman came and adopted me. I thought, "Wahoo! A family at last." These people took me home. I walked through their door and smelled . . . kids. (In fact, there were three kids, including one, Maggie, age eleven, who right now is writing down what I have to say.) They came and hugged me and kissed me and gave me a name—Portia.

Now I'm five. I've been with my family for a whole year. We take walks, eat delicious dog food (well, that's only me), and still visit my vet at shot and check-up time. I even have important jobs. I jump on my kids' beds every morning to wake them up. Sometimes their beds are so comfortable that I want to lay there all day. But I do have my own couch and blanket. Besides bones, what more could a dog ask for? I think one of my jobs is to run onto the school bus once in a while. The bus driver doesn't think so, takes me off, and calls me fat. Sometimes I just don't understand people.

My life is much better, and yours is too, because now you've heard my story.

PORTIA

70

NO BIGGER'N A MINUTE ("MINNIE")

Hi! My name is Minute, although I'm a little bigger than that. I live with my mom and dad. I think that I'm an only child—anyway, the only one who lives in the house—and I'm completely "rottenized."

My daddy sometimes calls me "Minute," and sometimes Mom calls me "Minnie Mouse." She calls me the perfect Chihuahua because I go to horse shows and everywhere else she goes. My horse-show friends call me a "halter Chi" since I'm so stout. My grandpa says that I'm a "buddy-size" Chihuahua. My uncle says that he wants to clone me. I guess that they're all pretty fond of me. I always fit in anywhere.

My hobbies are going to horse shows, drive-thru windows, the fetching of toys, and the playing of Can't-Catch-Me, where I have to be the one who is chased. I do a little singing too. Dad and I sing to the car radio, and we sing Happy Birthday a lot because everybody knows the words. For some reason they think that I have to hear the right words.

I never get tired of fetching toys. Sometimes I throw toys down the stairs and bark to let Mom know so that she can retrieve them. She seems to really like that. I'm a good sport. I let her have some fun too. Sometimes I have a hard time finding a toy that Mom or Dad wants to throw for me. I keep bringing them different toys. Finally it will be a good one, one that they like, and then I'll finally be able to throw it.

If only I could drive. I dream about driving up to windows and having those nice people just hand you all kinds of food. The Krystal is my favorite window. Mom and Dad try to fool me by saying, "Want to get some small square one?" But I know my Krystals.

When we go to horse shows, we always try to find—sometimes more than once a day—a drive-thru window. Shows are fun because I get to see and bark at other moms and dads. My mom rides in the arena, but friends and family members walk me around to visit. There's always a concession stand there. I guess that you've figured out by now that eating is one of my biggest pleasures. I know how to ask for food real cute. I try to talk (Arf! Arf!), which works about as well as "silent crying" (making my sides heave like I'm crying). My mom says, "Please don't cry, Minnie." That's when I know the food's coming.

Mom asked me if I wanted a friend, another Chihuahua. The thought of someone chasing me—I just love that game. It just makes me laugh out loud. Maybe my friend could run a little faster too. Mom was so worried that I might not be the favorite anymore. What if the new Chi took my place? I think that I'll be just as happy playing a little more fetch. I like being the favorite.

My mom says to me, "You're a gift from God. I prayed and prayed to find you—the perfect Chihuahua." I'm glad that I am the answer to her prayers.

MINNIE

72

CHARLIE BARROW
("MR. C")

My name is Charlie. I am a three-year-old, handsome English cocker spaniel. My first recollection of my mummy and daddy was when they decided to pick me from all those other doggies in the pet store. What a sign of relief when they picked me.

Mummy and Daddy are great. They treat me so well. Now I have managed to muscle my way onto the bed each night. Daddy treats me well. He takes me to the beach, as I love to swim, and I also get a real treat most Wednesdays when Daddy brings home my favorite from Basil's pizza.

I have had my problems. My big floppy ears have had infections, so Mummy or Daddy has to put medicine in my ears, and I hate it and usually go and hide, but Dr. Lester is great at the doggie hospital. I love to play sticks and balls, and I have a big back garden in which to roam around. I have a friend Jasper, who comes round and plays he is still a pup. He's bigger than me, which I don't understand. I think it's because he is a Lab, whatever that means.

A few years ago a new member to the family arrived—Baby Hannah. She is adorable and loves me so much. Mummy and Daddy are not from here. They keep going across some pond twice a year. I have to go to the pet hotel on Skidaway Road. Mr. Chip does me okay there, but I really miss Mummy and Daddy when they are gone.

Mummy started to call me "Mr. C" as she keeps telling me that I am her reenacted grandfather from England. I guess that's were that pond is.

Well, I need to go now as I just heard Daddy's Jeep come around the corner. I need to jump all over him and get all excited, then he might take me to seaside.

CHARLIE

MR. MURPHY MORRIS ("MURF")

Bonjour, mon amis! My name is Mr. Murphy, and I'm a bichon frise. My Uncle Tommy and Uncle Johnny, with whom I live, tell me that bichons are from France, so they have tried to teach me to bark in French. They both think that that trick is really cute, so I just try and go along with their joke. Their sense of humor sometimes goes right past me.

Anyway, I've lived with my two uncles now for almost a year. See, my mama is a really neat lady who helps all kinds of poor and underprivileged children; the governor called her up one day and said that he had to have her in Atlanta so she could work for children all over the state. I understood that the children needed her there, but we decided that it wasn't a place for a puppy. There are too many cars, too much noise, and too few sidewalks with trees and bushes for me to sniff. I miss her something terrible, but she comes to visit and she sends me neat gifts all the time.

Luckily Uncle Tommy and Uncle Johnny let me move in with them, and they are great. Uncle Tommy has an office at home, where he designs and decorates hotels and country clubs. I am a big help to him during the day. We have this plan worked out so that when his clients come in, I act really cute and adorable and demand (in a sweet way) their attention for as long as I can get it. Uncle Tommy charges by the hour, so if I can get them to play with me and keep them in the office longer, he makes more money. I also help keep his fabric samples warm by sleeping on them whenever he has them piled onto his worktable. Mostly, though, I just nap underneath his big desk.

Uncle Johnny and I play a lot together. He is a CPA, and helps charities all across Georgia so that they accomplish their good works and missions. He loves to have fun too and likes to travel. He takes me up to his house in the north Georgia mountains, and it is so neat. He has this noisy, rushing creek that he lets me play in (that water is cold) and a big, pretty meadow, where I chase butterflies during the day and lightning bugs at night.

The three of us live in a really handsome home in Ardsley Park with a cranky cat named Miss Ivana Plump. She is a white, domestic longhair, but to hear her tell it, she is the Queen of Sheba. I know I'm not supposed to say anything mean about anyone, but I tell the truth when I say she is one snotty kitty. Like the other day, Tommy and Johnny had a big party with lots of their fun friends over. I was in there with them all, having a blast. Where was Miss Plump? Hiding on top of an armoire, looking all put out. She says it is tacky having that many people in the house, and that she was sure some of them were riff-raff. Boy, is she hard to live with!

Well, that's about all I have time to say. Uncle Johnny and I are about to go to for a ride to the beach so that I can play with some sea gulls and run in and out of the waves. I'll probably get a hot dog, too. God bless you all, and take care. Bonsoir.

MURF

CHICCO ("FREACO")
AND
REILLY ("RI")

Hi! Our names are Chicco and Reilly. We live a block from Forsyth Park, where we spend most of our time. Our parents adopted us separately, but now we are siblings, with rivalry and everything. That means that an occasional good fight or two is not out of the question.

Now that you know who we are by our names, I guess we better tell you more about each of us. I am Reilly, the eldest; and if you will look at the picture, you can see me on the right. I am a cross between an American Staffordshire bull terrier and a boxer. Depending on my mood, I can be chasing a ball or teaching my younger brother who's in charge. Mom found me at the Humane Society in Savannah, and had planned to transfer me to a new life with her in Charleston. Thank God, the realtor types in Charleston didn't want me, so I stayed in Savannah with Dad. When Mom came down on the weekends, I was spoiled rotten with long walks, hot baths, and no sharing. Mom eventually moved back to Savannah. She still took me with her everywhere, from walks to the bank, to

78

meeting a friend for coffee at the gallery. I loved being an only dog; it meant I didn't have to share my part of the bed with anyone. Then Mom met Grace, a volunteer with AWARE. She brought Chicco to our household.

Hi! My name is Chicco. I'm on the left in the picture. As Reilly told you, Mom adopted me from Grace through a program called AWARE. Grace helped rescue me from a less-than-desirable home somewhere in Savannah. In my first few months I was stolen from Grace and returned after a short stint as a fighting dog. I love Grace, who brought me to meet my Mom and Dad at the PETsMART Adopt-A-Pet program. Unfortunately for Dad, another family wanted me and beat him to completing the adoption forms. Alas, I spent two weeks with my first adoptive parents before they decided (with my help) that it just wasn't going to work. Mom and I were blessed as she happened to stop by PETsMART and learned that I was available again. Grace, who lives up to her name, told Mom. The next day I was picked up from Doggie Daycare, and home I came.

When I first got to my home, Reilly and I had a few issues, mostly over food. "Humph," Reilly would say, "keep your mitts off my food, little boy." We worked it out though with a little behavior-modification intervention by my new parents. I was a growing boy that needed to assist.

Since then we've been one big happy family lounging in the park on sunny days, taking late-night romps, and teaching kids not to run up to strange dogs. Mom is really careful not to let us bounce on them when they do. There are so many places that we love to go to and things we love to do. I think the best thing, though, is knowing that we won't ever find ourselves back looking for a home or wondering where our next meal is coming from. That's for sure.

Yup, we know that we live where there are always biscuits in the cookie jar, toys to play with, a pat on the head, and a walk in the park. What else could a dog long for? Okay, see you next time in the park.

CHICCO AND REILLY

LACY ASHLEY
("HARD HEAD")

I was born in March 1995 in Decatur, Georgia, and a family with three young boys adopted me. Of course the mom had to take care of me. About ten months later the mom became pregnant with her fourth son, so she decided I needed to find another home. I couldn't blame her as she never had any time to herself. Anyway, through a friend of a friend I was adopted by my second mom, and we have been together ever since.

My new mom was pretty sad and needed someone to love her. She had lost her dad a few months before, and she was caring for her very ill mother plus working a full-time job. Sometimes, when things got really bad, she would sit and cry. I would immediately jump up on her lap and lick away the tears. This would make her laugh, and she would hug me and let me stay on her lap as long as she could. Eventually Mom had to put her mom in a nursing home to be cared for.

After a few months Mom decided to take me with her on a Saturday visit. I was a little scared because the door opened automatically when we got there; and then we got on an elevator, which was really weird. When we got off at the fourth floor, there were people all

81

around and some of them wanted to pet me. This was good; I like to be noticed. There were so many noises that I had never heard before that I barked a few times, but Mom said that it was okay and that I would get used to it. During my second visit two weeks later, I wasn't afraid anymore; and when I got off the elevator, I walked excitedly over to anyone wanting to pet me. From then on I enjoyed my visits as much as my new friends did. Then all of a sudden we didn't go anymore, and Mom was crying a lot again.

In 1998 we moved to Savannah, and Mom and I found that we both loved it here. We lived on Tybee for a while, and she would drive us down to the beach and we would sit in the car and watch the waves and the birds. I love to bark at birds. We had to sit in the car because Tybee has a law that no dogs are allowed on the beach.

A few months later Mom brought Spottee [see pages 83–84] home with her. I didn't like him at first, but now we get along okay as long as he understands I am the boss and he does what I say. Mom has a lot of love to give, and she shares it equally between us. We get a ride every weekend and enjoy seeing different areas of beautiful Savannah.

Thanks, Mom. I love you.

LACY

SPOTTEE ASHLEY ("COUCH POTATO")

As you can see from my girth, I am an eighty-six-pound couch potato. But life was not always this sweet.

One day in July 1998 it was hot and there was a light rain, and I was wandering around an industrial park trying to decide which way to go. I am not sure exactly how I came to be on the streets, but apparently I had been there for some time. I was very hungry, had two cuts on my body, and was covered in fleas and ticks. I was standing in the driveway when this lady drove up. She stopped the car, got out, and walked over to me. She gave me some petting and then said, "Go on home, boy."

I could tell that the lady wanted to help me, but something was holding her back. She got back in her car and went on up the driveway, where she parked. By the time she got out of her car I was standing behind it. She kept saying that she couldn't take me and that I needed to go home. She went in the building, but came back a few minutes later with some peanut-butter crackers and a bowl of water. I ate and then lay down in front of the glass door for a nap. She walked by the door three or four times during the afternoon, but did not come back out. At the end of the day the lady came out and told me to come with her. I jumped in the back of the station wagon and lay down.

We drove for a good while, and then we came to a hospital and she took me inside. The doctor examined me and said that I should stay overnight so that they could run tests. The people there did a lot to me that night, including four baths, but I sure felt better the next morning. My new mom picked me up that afternoon and took me home. This was the tough part because Mom was living with relatives and she already had Lacy, a cocker spaniel [see pages 81–82]. The relatives did not like dogs, but had tolerated Lacy. They were not happy to see me, but Mom kept saying she just could not leave me in the street.

During the next several months, Mom was told that she needed to find another home or get rid of me. So every weekend during the next several months Mom would put Lacy and me in the car and we would drive around Savannah for two to three hours looking for a home for the three of us. Eventually the relatives loosened up when we could not find a new home, and they agreed to let us stay awhile longer.

Although Lacy weighs a fourth of what I do, she bosses me around and is very jealous of any loving I get. But we enjoy our weekend rides around town and are both very lucky to have our mom, who almost lost her home rather than put me out on the streets again.

Thanks, Mom. Love,

SPOTTEE

TED-E SALTER ("DARLING DARLING")

I was born on November 21, 1990, two days before Thanksgiving. My mom's name was Muffin, a Lhasa-poo; and my dad, Booger, was a black chow. I had eleven brothers and sisters. I was the only buff-color. I was six weeks old when my now-parents adopted me. It was New Year's eve, and the firecracker noise that night really scared me. My parents put me in the bed with them to comfort me, and I've been there ever since. I've always looked like a cute, cuddly teddy bear—that's why my name is Ted-E.

My mom frequently was home with me during my first few years. She would hold me, rock me, and talk to me a lot. When she talks to me, she will say, "Ted-E, sit, I want to talk to you." I would sit and listen to her tentatively, turning my head as if to say, "Like okay, Mom, I hear what you're saying." We also like to play hide-and-seek.

I'm like a son to Mom. We love each other so much. I follow her every step. Mom went to work as a groomer five and a half years ago. She would take me to work with her. I would sit on a table next to her and watch. I enjoyed being with her. People would watch me through the windows. Some would come in the shop and ask about me. Others thought I wasn't real. When my mom would go out in the store, I would follow. People would stop us and pet me. Then they would ask what breed I was and say I still looked like a puppy. They can't believe I am more than eleven years old. My mom would tell them that it's all the TLC I received, also the good nutritional food.

We have a pool and I have a large tube with a lounge chair. Mom will push the tube up to the deck so that I can step down, sit in my chair, and float all over the pool. When I get too hot, I take a swim. Then I get back in my chair.

I became ill—passed blood—early this year. My vet changed my diet, and a urine sample was sent to Athens. X-rays and other tests revealed that I had a mass in my bladder. My mom attends a Bible class on Tuesday nights. She took me with her to pray for my healing. It was very cold that night. She put my red coat on (with an underside of black fur). It felt so good. They thought I was so cute. I just sat on my mom's lap and watched.

I had surgery in February to have the mass removed; it was as large as my mother's fist. The test proved positive, but Mom and her friends prayed for me. We believe that I am healed.

I am one of my mom's special joys in life. We also have four other dogs, all rescues, and two cockatiels.

Let me take this opportunity to tell people to please take care of their pets. So many are neglected and abused. I see this too often.

TED-E

BACARDE

My most favorite days are Saturdays, when both my mom and dad are home. They like to try and sleep late, but I'm determined to keep them on a regular timed schedule. There are lots of ways to wake them up, but I've found that standing on my mom's chest is the most effective. It's usually hard to ignore me and, besides, Saturday mornings are made for playing, not sleeping. I first picked out my parents the day they wandered into PETsMART thinking they would spend an hour just "looking" at all the dogs there before making a decision to take one home. I was determined to be the one they picked.

Putting on my most friendly and wide-eyed look, I went to work on Dad first. One look at my big brown eyes and a few minutes of my furious tail-wagging, and he was hooked. Humans can be so easy. After about an hour, I had my mom eating out of my hand—er, paw—as well. I was soon on my way to my new home. That was three years ago, and my parents' lives have never been the same. My mom tells me all the time what a smart dog I am, and I have to say, I agree. I

87

understand words like ball, play, walk, Mom, Dad, ride, treat, and toy. I've even started to learn how to put together the words my parents try to spell out. They still think I don't know what "t-r-e-a-t" or "r-i-d-e" means.

I'm also a big help around the house. Mom and Dad never have to worry about crumbs that fall onto the floor during dinner because I'm right there to clean them up. If it wasn't for me, think how messy the floor would get. I also like to sit up on the couch and supervise when dad vacuums the living room. I make sure he doesn't miss a spot.

Sometimes Mom, Dad, and I go for rides in the car. Usually we go to good places like the beach or to a restaurant. When I get to pick where we're going to eat, I always want to go to Sonic or McDonalds. They have the best hamburgers—no pickles or ketchup—and sometimes I get a cup of ice cream for dessert. I try to be neat, but somehow the ice cream always ends up all over my face.

My favorite thing to do is to go on walks. Sometimes I have so much energy when we come back inside that I do what my mom calls "doughnuts" around the house. I'm not sure what a doughnut is, but it must be a really good thing. My mom and dad always laugh at me when I'm running. They better be careful and stay out of the way. I will run them over if they get in the way.

Speaking of walks, I think I need to go and remind my mom that it's almost time for our nightly stroll. All in all, I think I picked the best parents in Savannah. Other people think I'm spoiled rotten. I think I'm just lucky.   BACARDE

OSCAR NOBLE

After reading *The Idiots' Guide to Jack Russell Terriers*, John and I took the plunge and added an ongoing wave of personality and energy to our petless home. Oscar joined us just a few weeks after we were married in August 2000. Our rough-coat puppy has provided us big adventures and daily entertainment.

Adventure number one occurred soon after Oscar arrived at our Wilmington Island home. At the time, our seven-foot wooden fence appeared sufficient to contain this seven-pound curious puppy. But . . . Oscar and Sammy (the sixty-five-pound mixed breed that lives on the other side of our fence) learned that after vigorously digging toward each other from their respective sides of the fence, a tunnel would form allowing Oscar to flatten out and crawl under. One day on Sammy's side of the fence, Oscar located the cat door and followed Sammy's cat-sister into the neighbor's house. Imagine the surprise of our neighbors when they returned home to find a puppy accident on their kitchen floor and Oscar resting peacefully on their sofa.

Now Oscar has a shock collar and stays at least a foot from the borders of the fence. This discipline lesson was much more painful for Oscar's owners than for him as he learned his new territory very quickly. Adventures aside, Oscar is a well-behaved dog who was easy to train. We credit Oscar's birth family, Elizabeth and Mark and their three Jack Russells in Ardsley Park, with making our job so easy. Oscar has been crate-trained since his beginning, and had received lots of positive guidance before coming to us when he was three months old. He still vacations at his birth family's home when we travel out of town and he's unable to join us.

Oscar jogs on the average about fifteen miles a week with me. During his two years of existence, Oscar has run at least a thousand miles with me, not to mention countless more miles in our backyard. He is a super running companion and always manages to outlast his human jogging partner. He has a keen eye for my running shoes and goes bananas when he sees me put them on. His intense excitement about running keeps me motivated too. Jack Russell enthusiasts are quick to say that Oscar will never be a good show dog because his chest has widened to accommodate his expanded lungs. But I feel quite certain that Oscar would choose running on the beach or sprinting though a lures course any day over participating in a dog show.

Overall, Oscar is a chase-anything, eat-anything dog who loves other animals and all people. He has an odd obsession with cardboard and prefers panty-hose containers, toothpaste boxes, and paper towel rolls to most other toys. Fortunately his technique for scanning the trash cans for these items does not involve tipping them over. And when the day is done, Oscar can relax and enjoy lazy time as well as any exhausted human. Oscar is an absolute joy who constantly provides unexpected twists in our daily household routine.

SHANNON NOBLE

BAILEY

No, I am not part chow, as some would think since my tongue is spotted black. I am *all* golden retriever, and you know what that means—trouble.

Ever since I was a very little puppy living in Colorado, I have always loved to chew things. Chewing holes in the carpet was always fun. Once I was old enough to reach onto the counters, I found some papers. Since Mom and Dad were nowhere to be found, I seized my opportunity, grabbed the stack of papers, and ran into the backyard, where I began to rip them into shreds. What fun to see bits of paper flying around the yard. Suddenly my dad came outside and started yelling—something about "taxes." I had no idea what he was talking about, but this tax thing must have been pretty important. Luckily my mom is very protective of me and told Dad to go inside and breathe. I don't think Dad liked me very much that day, but I am so cute that he got over it pretty quick. I don't bother with anything on the counters anymore.

Maybe that's why we moved to this place called Savannah, where we have wooden floors instead of carpet. I really like it here. We have a really great house downtown. I like to help decorate it by spreading the inside of pillows everywhere. I think it adds a certain flair. My mom disagrees and always picks it up. I will just have to redecorate again tomorrow.

One of the best things about living in Savannah is Forsyth Park. I love to go to the park. The park has all kinds of stuff for a big dog like me. Besides room to run around and other dogs to play with, it also has my arch-nemesis—squirrels. Those furry little rodent-like creatures with their fuzzy tails tease me constantly. They chatter away in their foreign language; and although I'm not sure what they're saying, I know they must be laughing at me. As soon as I see one, I zero in on my target and move stealth-like toward the nuisance. Slowly I tiptoe toward it, then when the moment is right, I try to ambush the little varmint. This is no easy task; it takes a lot of skill, concentration, and patience. Those darn things are as fast as lightning, so I have yet to catch one, but I will . . . one day, then they'll be sorry that they ever taunted me. After chasing squirrels, I feel very tired. As soon as we get home, I like to retire to my favorite napping place, the bathtub.

I'm glad we moved to this place, Savannah, because it seems like the perfect place for a dog. So the next time you're out walking in one of the squares, or in that park with the big white fountain—that they won't let me swim in—and you see a large golden retriever with a black-spotted tongue, that'll be me, Bailey, taking my mom for a walk on her leash.

BAILEY

SAM SCHWARTZ ("SAMMER-DO," "LOVIE," ("SWEET ANGEL")

It was so hot that day, the day she found me. So many others passed me by, probably thinking that I was dead or at least very close to death. The six giant turkey vultures slowly hovering and flying circles over me could have been the first clue to the passersby. Their second clue was probably the fact that I was literally skin and bones—twenty-three pounds on a fifty-pound frame, and virtually no hair.

I saw her drive by, slow down, and then keep going. I was running, galloping along the right hand side of the road, going nowhere fast. I'm not sure why I was running or to where, maybe just running away from myself. A few minutes later, she returned. The car stopped, and there she was, offering me some crushed ice from her fountain soda and a banana. Like when I'm this far gone some monkey food will help me.

I don't remember much about the next few days. I just know that for the first time I felt safe. She scooped me up in a soft, pink T-shirt, gently put me into the car, put some cool air-conditioning on me, and told me that she wouldn't hurt me. I fell right to sleep. I must have really been in bad shape to fall asleep next to a perfect stranger. But you must understand, it was 120 degrees on the road that July day in Appling County on Highway 144. It gets worse.

Within the next few days, I slowly learned to trust her. She told me over and over that I would never know pain, hunger, fear, or helplessness again; and there was something about her ways that made me know for sure that this would be a lasting friendship.

Soon thereafter I met another key person in my life. Her name is Stephie. She's my doctor. She is the one who discovered that the reason green fluid was oozing from the left side of my mouth and that there was systemic infection was because my jaw was badly broken. They assumed that I was hit by a car, and indeed I had been. But that was not the cause of my shattered jaw. I had been shot at close range with a shotgun. My lower left jaw had a two-inch space of missing bone, the point that took most of the force of the shot. My mom doesn't know why I was shot, and I really don't remember much about that day, but she told me that she likes to think it was just an accident.

For two years I had a steel plate in my jaw, until the bone graft from my left arm grew into a new lower left jawbone. Now all the infections, medications, and checkups are over. I've been living in Savannah for almost four years now. My life is grand.

I know I have a past, but please don't feel sorry for me. I have known pain, but I have also known great joy. I am more loved and valued than I ever could have hoped for. I know this is true because Momma tells me every day that I am her sweet angel. I think she's pretty special too.

SAM

**PRECIOUS
MCNEILL
SMITH**

Life in Savannah with Mom-Mom and Deda, my masters, started on a very cool February 14. Boy, it was a long ride to Macon, Georgia. It all began for two very special little girls who are granddaughters to my family. Ansley and Kelsey, ages five and three years, love me in an extraspecial way. You see, Ansley and I have personalities very much alike. We like to run, jump, holler, rock and roll, or just cuddle. And, of course, I do a lot of digging and barking.

After Sissi, Mom-Mom and Deda's Lhasa apso, went to paradise, it was decided that Deda, who had given fourteen years of true love to Sissi, needed another puppy, and that the girls would benefit by a learning relationship with a new dig.

After they had looked long and hard for a Westie, they heard about me in Macon. Bright and early, Mom-Mom, Deda, and Ansley—loaded with goodies and books—set off on the pick-up ride. Ansley was looking forward to a baby puppy. She was all strapped in with Mom-Mom in the backseat, and there was a big wicker basket with a soft blanket and a teddy bear for me.

As they proceeded west there was singing, the playing of games, giggling, and eating of goodies. Mom-Mom and Ansley were getting restless, so the vehicle had to take a stop for R&R. Back again on the road, Ansley said, "Deda, we're in the deep forest, aren't we?" Just think, all those pine trees on the roadside to get to where I was born.

After they arrived at my location, there were giggles as I tried my best to be so cute for them. I was the last of five puppies and I needed a home. Ansley was so excited about me that she shouted, "Deda, isn't she so precious." So here I am, one year old now and extremely happy. And my name is Precious.

My family also has an Alaskan malamute that just strayed in to stay one December day. Queen is her name as she royally took Mom-Mom's heart and soul. Queen weighs a hundred pounds. She loves me and lets me wallow all over her. We run and chase each other several hours daily. I also live with a twenty-one-year-old Siamese cat. If I'm careful and don't get caught, I can eat his food. We lie together in the sun and just watch out the window for our girls to come play with us.

PRECIOUS

MISS
BIRDIE
("BIRDIE")

I am a three-year-old Labrador-shepherd mix. I met my best friend, Caroline, and her cat, Moose, two years ago when she moved to my neighborhood. I lived with someone else before I adopted Caroline. She would feed me and let me come inside her house. Sometimes I would find her at work and jump into her car and stay there until she clocked out. A couple of times she even saved me from the dog-catcher.

I have many human friends who let me come and visit them. They always give me treats. I also have some canine friends who come over to play with me; or, if they live near me, I sometimes go to visit them.

Ms. Caroline always takes me for a walk so I can swim after the ball or play in the marsh chasing the fiddler crabs. I love to swim and get muddy. Show me a mud puddle and I am in it. The only bad thing about it is that I also get washed off.

I also love children, especially Caroline's nephew, Erik. He is so much fun to be around. When he comes over, I know that we are in for some fun. We go for bike-rides, play keep-away with a toy or ball, or go roller-blading. Once he had me on the leash when I saw a squirrel, so I took off for the chase, with Erik rolling right behind me. He finally let go of the leash and rolled into the grass. I did not catch the squirrel, but, hey, a gal's gotta do what a gal's gotta do.

But my favorite thing in the world is when Caroline takes me for a ride in the car. I love going places. Sometimes we ride past a big open field with these strange-looking animals. (What are "cows" anyway?)

I always like coming home after all of my fun. I couldn't have asked for anything better than to be with Ms. Caroline. Life is good.

Love,

MISS BIRDIE

MAGGIE
WATSON
KARLISS

Hi there, I am a tricolor basset hound. I am also Sherlock's big sister. He already told his story in the first *Savannah Dogs* [see pages 73–74]. I know because my mom told me. It is now time for me to tell my story, so here I go.

It all started about a year ago when I needed a home. I feel very special, because our human parents picked me even after I had passed through the adorable, cute stage when my ears and paws were bigger then the rest of me. My new parents decided Sherlock needed a sister-playmate. If truth be known, I feel it was also because he was spoiled, and they knew it. He was going on three and had been the only "pup" in the house until I came along. Needless to say, he was very, very spoiled and did not like sharing. He especially did not like sharing our parents in the beginning of our relationship.

I can vividly recall the first day we met. It took place in a neutral location, our very own Colonial Cemetery. Why there? Well, that could be another story in itself. I'll save that one for *Savannah Dogs III*. We were both on our leashes. I was attempting to behave like a lady. After all, I was older. I guess you could also describe my behavior as somewhat shy. Sherlock, on the other hand, was attempting to do the typical dog-greeting things. I know all you canine readers out there know what I am referring to without me elaborating. Anyhow, I was not too happy about meeting him. When I realized our mom was taking me into her car with him, I became somewhat anxious. I was glad she put me in the passenger's seat next to her. I sat up as tall as I could, attentively watching exactly where we were going so I could find my way back just in case I needed to.

Well, we finally arrived home. As I walked around the house I saw a basket on the floor overflowing with chewies and toys. Also on the floor were more chewies and toys. I could tell I had my job cut out for me. It was time for Sherlock to learn about sharing.

From that moment on, whenever I would go over and attempt to help myself to a chewy or toy, Sherlock would stop whatever he was doing, come over to me, and take whatever I had away from me. He could have several chewies and toys in front of his big paws. It did not matter. Mom even got me my very own basket and toys. That did not matter either. As far as he was concerned, what was his was his and what was mine was also his. He always wanted whatever I had—typical behavior for a younger brother. Being "the new kid" in the house, I did not resist. I just let him have whatever I had. However, if I do say so myself, I have a pretty good memory. I just took it all in and bided my time.

Finally I had taken enough of his selfishness. One weekend, when we were all visiting Aunt Rosie, Uncle Jim, and Cousin Max—the latter of whom, by the way, is a dachshund in central Florida—I had my chance to teach Sherlock his first lesson in sharing. Cousin Max,

Sherlock, and I were alone in the den. I thought to myself, Here is my big opportunity to finally get back at Sherlock and help him learn about sharing. Max is not much for chewies; he was taking a siesta on the couch. Sherlock was doing his usual thing, trying to keep all the chewies and toys for himself. I decided to grab one and make a run for it. I knew he would chase me. We ran around and around the room until I became tired. I dropped the chewy to make Sherlock think I had given in, as I always had in the past. I then jumped up on the love seat and sat down in order to catch my breath. Bassets are not known for their endurance. I guess it is our short legs. Sherlock completely collapsed on the floor beneath me. When I thought his eyes were closed, I carefully made my move. I jumped off the love seat and into the air toward him. I know some of you out there have heard of the "flying nun," well meet the "flying basset." My ears were straight out from my head and parallel to the floor, my legs were completely stretched out, and I was in flight. I was just landing on his back as everyone came into the room. My dad now refers to that day as the time I "Pearl Harbored" Sherlock.

Sherlock still needs some work on sharing. Now, however, he will let me play with a chewy or two on occasion. Being the big sister, I feel the need to continue helping my little brother learn about sharing. So whenever he starts showing signs of extreme selfishness, I play my little game of chase. Wish me luck. I will need it.

MAGGIE

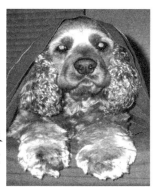

CAYENNE PEPPER
KERKOSKI
("KY," "KYKY")

My name is Cayenne as in cayenne pepper, but I also go by KyKy. I would prefer to be called "the princess" as I am treated like royalty . . . as I should be. Besides my daily vitamins, I also expect and receive nummies (treats) several times throughout the day. I insist on only drinking fresh water from the bathroom sink. Why my mommy continues to leave out a bowl of stale water for me, I will never know. She should know that I would dehydrate first before I have to drink from a bowl. Yuck! Doesn't everyone drink water straight from the bathroom sink?

I hate it when my family has to leave me each day for work. I always wish to go, but I only insist when they are wearing their weekend casual clothes. If I don't get to go, from the front window I regretfully watch them leave. When my family returns home, I do expect a lot of loving to make up for the abandonment. I do feel that my mommy gets a little carried away sometimes. She tends to want to hold and hug me forever. All I can think about while I am being victimized is, "Ah, jeez! How much longer is she going to love on me?" But I have to remind myself that of course she wants to love on me—I can't help it that I am so wonderful. On the other hand, my daddy shows me his love by playing chase with me throughout the house. No one in particular ever announces the beginning of the race, but there usually is a mutual agreement of a winner. I will let you in on a little secret—I usually let him win.

My favorite pastime is sleeping the day away. I love it when Mommy and Daddy get to spend the day with me and all they want to do is sleep. That's the best to me. When I am not sleeping, I become the protector of the house. I feel it is my responsibility to monitor the yard. Those squirrels must not be allowed into the yard. You see, I must protect my family from these very dangerous squirrels. Before my family can even enter the yard, I must inspect the squirrel routes to run off any potential threat. All this protection I provide is very exhausting. So the majority of the time I just try to observe the squirrels from several windows throughout the house. To be honest, I am usually shaking all over with excitement when I spot an intruding squirrel. To the untrained eye it would appear that I am freezing, but truly I am torn between two emotions—should I chase the squirrel or should I observe it while I'm lazily perched here at my window? I do, however, get embarrassed when I am caught being a bit lazy. I usually play it off as if the squirrel just appeared in the yard, and then I proceed to fall all over myself trying to get out the dog door to chase the annoying squirrel away.

Ah, jeez! My life sure can be difficult. Is there anyone out there willing to change places with me?

CAYENNE

SHAYNA KING

I'll tell ya, life is good. Well, at least since I came to live with my new mom and dad. I'm very thankful that they adopted me. I mean, with all the Taco Bell hype I thought I'd wind up as an underpaid, overworked stunt double. But my green eyes, long coat, and human-like eyelashes ensured me a more stable future. At that time I was living with my biological mom and dad, along with my four brothers. We were quite young, only a few weeks old to be exact. Word around the playpen was that there was a well-written ad in the newspaper advertising our availability. I guess I could understand, we were a bit rowdy to all be living in one single residence. But the Taco Bell complex once again had me worried. I thought, Who would want a dog that eats chalupas? But really, I don't even like salsa, I swear. Hoping the stereotype wouldn't haunt me for the rest of my life, the front door opened. I had to dart at the newcomers, along with my brothers. That's when I met this friendly young couple. Grabbing their attention would be a task, but being the only female in the bunch . . . I had that going for me. We took turns jumping in their laps, trying to win them over. But I had a feeling only one of us would sleep good that night, and I was determined to be the lucky one. I fluttered my eyelashes, wagged my tail, and then flopped over on my back. That always gets them.

Well, it did. And I was right. That night I slept like a king. When they took me home, it was like walking into a toy store. There were bones, stuffed animals, squeaky things, and some real tasty treats. From that point on, well, I knew I could get away with whatever I wanted, so long as I perform a few tricks here and there, on command of course.

It took a few days to get acclimated to the new house. But I eventually learned the layout. I have my very own bedroom, my very own backyard (with my select choice of places to do business, if you know what I mean), and a mom and dad that like to go for really long walks. My bedroom comes complete with cozy sleeping quarters. My backyard keeps me busy for hours, with all the square footage of leaves and grass a puppy could ever want. And those long walks are just that—long, satisfying walks. Oh, I can't forget the beach. They love the beach. And yes, you guessed it, I really love the beach too. Sand tastes so good.

I'm cute, small, and very lovable, if I do say so myself. But I never thought I'd stumble upon such a wonderful life. Being a puppy is fun, but being a king is even better. And let me reiterate—life is good.

SHAYNA

EASY MICHAEL FERGUSON DENHAM ("EASY")

I had just bought a house, had the yard fenced, and determined that it was time that I was ready to commit to having a pet—a dog specifically. I was working at a local hospital, where a physical therapist, Nancy Hulley, was also involved in animal rescue efforts in the Savannah area. When I told her that I needed to find just the right companion, she asked me for a list of characteristics that I sought in a dog in order that she could start the quest.

Being the obsessive character that I am, I took my assignment seriously and dashed off a list: must be small, female, gentle, fun, easygoing. For weeks we went to animal viewings and visited dogs in foster care. After each visit I felt tremendous guilt for not taking a dog home, but none was the right one.

A month or so later, one Saturday morning, Nancy called me. "There's a dog in trouble in a foster home," she announced. "I'd like to drive you up to the country to take a look at him. He's not exactly what you said you 'wanted,' but I have a feeling about this," she said. Off we drove in her two-seater car to meet up with the dog at a mini-mart somewhere between Savannah and

Oliver, Georgia. En route, Nancy explained that the dog's name was Easy. He had been abandoned by his owner and then placed in foster care. Because he was already weak and sick when he had been placed in foster care, the other dogs had ganged up on him, beat him up, and prevented him from eating.

We pulled off the two-lane road at the appointed location and settled down to await his arrival. Nothing could have prepared me for what happened next. A car drove up, the car door opened, and the dog—with head hung down—crawled out. He dragged himself to a grassy area and promptly passed out. He was unimaginably thin, dirty, and covered with wounds. "You can think about it for a few days," the foster parent offered. But I had already made up my mind. I was hooked. I couldn't send him back. And knew in my heart that if I delayed my decision, he would be dead in a few days.

So we all piled into Nancy's car. Easy and I were crammed into a seat together, and he was so big that this was a challenge. Our first visit was the vet's office to get him checked out. While there, he passed out again on the examining table, and the vet commented that rarely had he seen such a depressed dog, but believed that with care and attention Easy would survive. We bathed and cleaned him up and discovered that Easy was a three-year-old blue tick hound–shorthaired pointer combination.

To make a very long story short, Easy and I have been together for eight years now, and I have to report that he is absolutely the best friend and companion that a girl could have. It took a while for him to come into his own, but he has shown himself to be a wise old soul with a great sense of humor.

No, he's not the small female dog that I thought I wanted when I set out on this odyssey. But he is everything that I needed plus some. He is a gentle being who continues to bless and enrich my life, and I am so very grateful for him.

KAY DENHAM

LYNDALE M'LORD RILEY ("RILEY")

It's been said that I live "the life of Riley," and I admit, my staff take very good care of me. But not to be immodest, I really believe I deserve the very best of treatment. From the time I was a puppy I have always tried to exhibit good manners and have never chewed up a pair of shoes nor anything else for that matter, only a stray Kleenex or two, but then those don't really count. The kitchen door was a mistake, I admit, but when they left that evening, I was overcome with a regrettable and in retrospect unjustified panic, thinking they would not return.

Nor have I ever hopped up on the furniture, beds included, though there was that one time when my male caretaker had cut himself chasing me in the middle of the night. It seemed to me that it was my obligation to provide comfort and reassurance by curling up next to him for the night, and I bore no lasting grudge for being summarily deposed.

There have been one or two minor lapses from grace, but surely unwrapping a one-pound Christmas box of chocolates was a small price to pay for my years of devotion to their needs—waking them early, seeing to it that they are up and about at an respectable hour, taking them on daily walks, and bringing balls for them to throw in order to keep them fit and in shape. How was I to know it was not one of my presents?

Though I don't really enjoy them, I have been a model of tolerance about the periodic boat trips in which I agree to participate albeit reluctantly. Besides the challenge of leaping up onto a narrow deck from a dock three or more feet below without banging my head, it's not easy going for long hours without even a blade of grass anywhere in sight much less an accessible plot of land when I am in need. But I don't begrudge them these cruises as it gives me an opportunity to broaden my outlook on the world with exciting new places and lots of interesting people to meet.

I have made it very clear that I don't enjoy Agility Training. I figure that I am sufficiently agile to meet whatever challenges life has in store for me. Nor did it ever make much sense to me to run up a steep plank and down the other side for no particular reason that I could ever fathom. On the other hand, I am withholding judgment on "Obedience Training." While I figure that I am obedient within the parameters of my own priorities, I do enjoy the walks, and therefore I will put up with heeling, as an example, unless a squirrel needs exercising or I spot another walker to whom I must extend the normal courtesy of greeting. Good behavior does brings its own rewards; most strangers appreciate a polite acknowledgment of their presence and usually reciprocate with a lovely ear rub and at the least a pat on the head. Those who don't, I ignore and do not intrude upon.

In short, the life of Riley is a good one.   RILEY

111

HUNTER, LORD OF WHITEMARSH

I was born on January 3, 1993, on Hunter Army Airfield in Savannah, Georgia. When I was a few months old, I went to live with my new family, Angie and Doug Connell, on Whitemarsh Island. I knew from the start that fate had brought me to this island.

Life as the Lord of Whitemarsh started by learning my new domain. My new mother, Angie, took me on long walks all around the island. Sometimes I made the whole walk, and other times I only made half the walk and had to be carried for the trip home. The walks gave me the opportunity to not only take in the lay of the land, but to meet those who lived on Whitemarsh. We walked mostly in the afternoons or early mornings without regard to the season. I will always cherish these walks and the time I spent with Mommy.

As I got older I gained more confidence and freedom. As soon as the chance presented itself, I would make a dash out of the gate and sometimes be gone for hours. I would chase squirrels, swim in Richardson Creek, or just flop around in the marsh. My family usually was so happy to see me that they would actually drive out to pick me up from my excursions and then promptly give me a shampoo, bath, and combing.

When I reached my dog teens, I decided that it was time to take Angie to obedience school. I figured that if she was to be my walking companion then I had better get her trained while she was young. We attended several weeks of training and made good progress. She was learning the proper way to address me and how to correctly hold her leash. The training was not too difficult, and Angie was a quick study. Needless to say, we graduated at the top of our class.

The years following Angie's obedience training were filled with change. In November 1994 Mommy and Daddy had a baby girl named Rachel and quickly followed up in January 1997 with another baby girl, Morgan. Both girls were beautiful, small, and loud. They did very little but sleep, eat, and cry the first year or so, but they were my responsibility. I was there for love, comfort, protection, and play whenever it was needed. At that time I realized that my size made it difficult for the girls to learn to walk. They were constantly bumping into me and falling down. I knew that they would need more space, so I took up temporary quarters in the backyard guesthouse. Although these conditions were not what I was used to, I accepted this change without complaint. I knew this was in the best interest of my family.

In the past two years I have once again taken quarters in the main house. I am older now, but still make my daily rounds around Whitemarsh. I spend most days in my daddy's recliner, relaxing and conserving my energy. In the afternoon, when everyone is home safely, I check the neighborhood, run and play with some of the neighbor kids, sniff around for any interlopers, still take the occasional swim or marsh frolic, and generally carry out the duties of the elder statesman of White-marsh.

Life is great for me. I have a wonderful, loving family, a lovely home, great friends, and great neighbors. I spend warm, sunny days outside in the sunshine, and cold, rainy days in the warm, cozy house. I love my family and they love me. Who could ask for a better way to spend one's life?

HUNTER

BAKER

My name came from a Baker's brand unsweetened baking chocolate box. My mistress is a chocoholic and is constantly making brownies—the kind with nuts in them. She decided that Baker was a good strong name for me. Some people assume with that name that I am male, but I'm not. In fact, now that I had that little operation at the crazy vet's office, I have a scar on my bubble-gum belly, and male dogs don't get as excited when they play with me as they used to.

I have one other scar. A big black dog took a bite out of my left eyebrow when I was little. I was taken by surprise. It was bloody. But my mistress didn't whisk me off to get stitches and soon it healed. Now you can hardly tell unless you look very close. I sometimes play with that same big black dog at the puppy party we have in our neighborhood every night.

My father was a hunter and my mother was a show dog. I'm not as large as most chocolate Labs, which suits my mistress just fine. My tail is cocktail-table height, so when company visits I can knock over their iced tea glasses easily.

I was a surprise Christmas present. When I was only

seven weeks old, this really big guy, Jared, scooped me up from my brothers and sisters and brought me to my mistress' house. He deposited me in the middle of a really big bed, where she found me when she came home from church. Boy, was she surprised. I could tell. I had to train her a little, but she caught on fast. And now we're really happy with each other—you should hear the words of wisdom she spouts to me. I don't get to sleep in her big bed though.

Now don't get me wrong, I love my mistress, but boy, she does some strange things. She attaches me to this hot pink string and pulls me all over the neighborhood. I could do without the string. What I really love to do is run after squirrels. I'm really fast if I do say so myself. But those squirrels always get away from me. They can go up trees and I haven't mastered that yet. I'm pretty athletic. I can jump high to catch frisbees. I forever can retrieve tennis balls and sticks, especially when someone throws them in the water. My Uncle Henry helped me learn to retrieve whole tree limbs in the water. And I love to shake off the water on the throwers. They seem to like it too because they jump and scream.

I'm now a mature three years old, but when I was a puppy I loved to chew things. One time I discovered the good taste of vinyl flooring and chewed a chunk of it off the hall floor. I had chewed up a good part of the hall floor, when my mistress got somebody to take it all away. In its place is this very slippery wood floor. I can't chew it, but when it's hot outside it is cool to lie on.

I'm proud to say that I'm responsible for another home improvement project. In our backyard I dug up a huge patch of grass exposing all that wonderful-to-roll-in dirt. Again though, my mistress took away my fun and brought in a lot of pieces of dirt with grass growing out of them. She also, I think, told me I better not try to chew this new grass or else.

I have been to school because my mistress is a real education freak. I learned to sit, stay, heel, and jump through hoops. I was not the star of the class, but I was also not the dumbest. I graduated with a respectable certificate, though I probably could use some graduate work.

My mistress believes in exposing me to a lot of culture. I've traveled up and down the entire East Coast, I've roamed the streets of New York City, swum in the cold and warm Atlantic Ocean, sailed on boats, ridden on elevators, and dug in the snow. I've eaten caviar, vinyl as I said, bacon, pizza, and bourbon balls. I've attended elegant dinner parties.

My playmates are Vincent II [see pages 30–32] and Midnight. Vinny is a golden retriever who loves being where I am and running interference when I'm on my leash. Midnight is the black cat next door. He's had a checkered past and loves to taunt me. He sits on the brick wall looking down at me, but never wants to play like Vinny does. What is it with these cats?

The picture above shows me modeling a designer collar made by Gene Carpenter. Pretty neat, don't you think?

BAKER

ZOE SMITH
("ZIP,"
"MISS BROWN")

I was born on Mother's Day, four years ago, along with a noisy, pushy crowd of brothers and sisters. Of course I was one of the loveliest. I have a soft honey-colored coat with an undercoat of shimmering blonde highlights. I doubt if a master colorist at the finest of professional salons could achieve such a golden hue. My ears are like silk, and I have soft and soulful eyes. I believe my beauty contributed to the fact that I was the first to be chosen to leave the squirming and wiggling mass of siblings.

On a hot day in July, while resting in the sun, a shadow fell over me and my family. When I looked up, there was a smiling face above me looking at the group. I immediately pushed and climbed my way to the front of the pen where I lived. I had to be chosen by this smiling girl. I was a little startled when my feet left the ground and I was lifted high into the air by this girl. She held me close, and I heard her say, "I will take her on a trial basis." I didn't know what that meant, but I was happy to be near this human. We hopped into her car, and she put me on the seat next to her. "You will make the perfect gift," she said, and then she began to tie a large red satin bow around my neck. Off we went. I couldn't see out of the car, but it was cool inside and I knew I looked even more lovely with my bow.

We stopped at a house, and the girl scooped me up and took me inside. There was a much older girl. I was plopped down on the bed by her, but she didn't seem to be pleased to see me. "What is this?" she said. "It is a gift for you," my girl said. Then I realized that I was the gift, and I panicked, wetting the bed. This was not the way to make a good first impression. The "old girl" picked me up and looked in my face for a long while. I gave her my best dog smile. She must have thought I was beautiful because we have been together for four years now. My old girl put up with my wild first year, the dog equivalent of the terrible twos. I went to obedience school, and needless to say I wasn't the valedictorian. I grew like a weed, becoming clumsy with long gangly legs. As I grew taller and stronger, I found my calling in life. I noticed that my old girl was slow and had trouble standing at times. When we walked she could never keep up. I heard her say she had rheumatoid arthritis. Now I could help her. On mornings that she has trouble standing, I stand by her bed, brace my long legs, and then she uses my strong back to help her stand. When she is sitting in her chair, I sit close with my head on her knee and she exercises her painful hands by petting my head and scratching my ears.

I am still a beauty, but my real purpose in life is to be a best friend and a wonderful nurse. Beauty isn't forever, but the love of a good friend lasts through time. (I have to admit, though, I still wear a red collar to show off.) A very good dog,

ZOE

JOEY
("BABY JOEY,"
"LITTLE MAN")

I am a beagle–basset hound–shepherd mix. People fall in love with me immediately because I have sad puppy-dog eyes, soft velvety ears, big meaty paws, and a long body like the slinky dog in *Toy Story*. I'm a little shy and sometimes afraid of people, but I love the attention.

I was born in Charlotte, North Carolina, and some-how made my way to the dog pound with my five brothers and sisters. We were saved by a rescue group, Project Halo, and taken to a foster home. We went to PETsMART every weekend to find permanent homes. I was the last one to find a family, but I knew my per-fect mommy and daddy were coming to get me. One day my mom and dad appeared, and I jumped up on the pen and licked my mom's face. When they took me out of the pen, I lay down between my mom's feet and then my dad's feet, and they fell in love with me. They knew it was my way of telling them that I wanted to go home with them.

I slept a lot when I first got to my new home and would not leave my mom and dad's side. I couldn't even walk up the stairs for the first few weeks because

I didn't know how. I got confused because my daddy's putting green looked like grass, and I thought that was where I was supposed to go to the bathroom. My mom and dad spoil me rotten. They take me to PETsMART for new treats all the time and let me sleep on the bed with them. I even have my own pillow.

I was pretty scared when we first moved to Savannah. There's lots of traffic and loud noises. I don't like anything with wheels. I howled all the time when I was alone and hated to go outside. My mom says I have anxiety issues and my vet, Dr. Christiansen, put me on some medication for a little while. I'm feeling much better now.

I love to go to Forsyth Park and play with my friends. I'm pretty happy-go-lucky, so any dog at the park is my friend. I like to run and have the other dogs chase me. My mom and dad love it because they think it will tire me out and help me to sleep through the night. I like to get up at least twice a night to check things out. My mom says it's because I have a stronger will than she does and she would rather take me outside than listen to me whine all night. Whining is very effective in helping me get what I want.

I'm only a year old and still learning a lot about life. I was even afraid of the candle on my ice cream at my first birthday party. I'm just glad my mom and dad found me that day at PETsMART. They may think that they picked me, but I really picked them. I wish all little orphaned dogs were as lucky as I am.

JOEY

ROXY BORDEN ("ROXY DOODLE")

I remember it was like yesterday. My father was diagnosed with cancer in November 2000. He and my mother had moved from Pennsylvania to Savannah to be closer to my husband, to me, and to their grandchildren, Alexandra and Andrew. They lived with us for a short while and moved into a house in Guyton just before he was diagnosed with this awful disease.

Every chance that I had was spent visiting my father. In conversation with my mother she mentioned the small puppy that frequented her burnt garbage pile in the backyard. Dad would laugh because he said the puppy was modest. The puppy would only do her business in the woods behind the tall grass. Mom and Dad saw the puppy almost every day pass by their yard. Mom said the puppy wasn't more than three months old.

I thought about this puppy quite often and wondered if it belonged to anyone. Since this creature was so little, I knew that it could not survive the cold winter temperature or fend off any wild animals that would come its way. I was also concerned about the busy road close to where my mother lived. Surely this little pup was surviving by luck. It was now the third week of January, and it seemed to rain every day. My father's health was getting worse, and when he saw the puppy it would make him smile. A good meal, a good bath, and a nice warm towel from the dryer would fix her right up. At home I then had a Great Dane and two loving "Savannah setters" at home that I had rescued, but I was sure that I could make room for one more.

Dad had many trips to the hospital to receive chemotherapy, and it made him very tired. I was very upset that my father might not recover from cancer. One night while visiting I decided to step out back and enjoy the beauty God put on this earth. Anyway, I heard some rustling over in the garbage pile. There she was—wet, hungry, and full of life. I've never seen a tail wag like hers. Picture a sidewinder treading water or an inchworm trying to make its way sideways. Her whole body wiggled back and forth. She had a small rock and some chewed-up tinfoil hanging from her mouth. I cautiously bent over and petted her. It was hard to tell if she was a purebred because she was so little. She had one ear that stood straight up in the air. It looked to be bigger than her head. The other ear came halfway up and then flopped. Her eyes were big and brown. She was beautiful.

So much has happened since that cold January night. Roxy—she got her name from the night she tried to eat rocks as food—is a purebred German shepherd. She has a wonderful home with my husband, my children, and me. She gets along great with all of her brothers and her sister, except when she's eating noodles, her favorite food. She now is one year of age and has had a knee operation because of hip dysplasia. Roxy takes medicine every day for her hips and joints, and is doing wonderfully. My father did pass away in March of 2001. I thank the Lord for sending Roxy our way to make our days and lives brighter. She continues to spread love and joy. There will always be a special place in my heart and home for her.

JACQUELINE BORDEN

GINGER BOVEE
("STINKS")

Well, I may not look it, but I am really happy. I am the grandpuppy of two grandparents that do not know that I am a dog instead of a human, but I will not tell them any differently. We will keep this our little secret, okay? I was born March 31, 1997, into an AKC-certified family of basset hounds. Some of my first memories include being placed inside a cage with my brother and sister puppies and transported to the local flea market. My momma walked up to my cage, took one look at my human-looking, sad eyes and was hooked. She knew by the size of my paws that I was going to be big later on. Now, sixty pounds later, I did not disappoint.

My life has come a long way from that early flea-market period. When Mommy goes to work each day, I get immediate attention from my grandparents. Whenever they travel up to Blichton to tend their large garden on their land there, they always take me with them. I would make a good farm doggie—I always look forward to walking up and down the growing rows of produce, protecting the garden from harmful rodents and nosey birds. Yes, sir. Without me that garden would not make it. My grandparents don't have to worry about losing me out there in their garden. To find me, all they have to do is look for my pointed tail wagging in the sunshine.

Even though I may be a hero out there on the farm, there is someone who doesn't find much respect for me—my grandparents' calico cat, Weezie. Born in the wild, she is still quite restless; and, try as I might, she won't let me be her friend. As a matter of fact, she's really mean to me. Early on, I found out that those razor-looking things on the end of her paws can really hurt. Now, if she just looks at me the wrong way, I yelp, tuck my tail, and haul off running. I am trying not to let the abuse I take from her mold my psyche and ego in the least, but it's very hard.

Every Monday night our local fire station has a practice run. Their big red fire truck lets out a loud siren. Being quite competitive, I always try to out-sound the fire truck. I tilt my head back, pucker my lips, and let out my I'm-a-hound-dog-howling-at-the-moon howl. I proudly stroll back into my house afterwards because that big fire truck is always the first to back down when it hears me howl.

Other than walking the rows in the garden, do not expect me to do much more work. I prefer air-conditioned comfort in the summer time and a warm, heated house in the wintertime. My goodness, down here in the South the summertime can be quite exhausting. So I make sure that my spots that are under the air-conditioner vents and the ceiling fans are quite secure. Well, that's all I've got for now, but I'll keep you posted.

GINGER

126

GRETA

September 1999. We buried Greta today. I have to admit that I didn't want to come. It is much easier to go about the day, forcing the inevitable into the back of your mind, and receive the news in the quiet comfort of your own home after the day is done, distant and un-feeling. It's only a phone call after all. No red, tear-filled eyes to look into. No one extending a warm hand to ease the pain that you don't really want to admit you have anyway. Just bury it away . . . that's what I told myself, but I knew I had to be there. I loved her too much.

Greta was, in fact, loved by many. Everyone she met became an instant friend. Her eyes were bright. Her lips almost always curled into that smile that let even the most remote of strangers know that she was glad to see them. Heck, she was downright ecstatic to get to know you. The first sight of her could be intimidating—the strength, the confidence. I've seen more than a handful of people take a step back, their faces dropping cold, as she made her quick approach. Even in their fear you could see admiration and respect. But soon she was on them, and anyone who knew her, especially those of us who loved her, had to grin at the event about to unfold: relief washing over the faces, involuntary sniffles followed by the physical affection of long-lost companions. Another stranger would be taken in, and a new friend would be made.

On this day, however, there would be only family. I drove to my parents' house in the morning not really sure of what to expect or how I would react to what was to take place. The outcome was certain, but the process was gray. I felt nothing at the time, no real sadness or heightened emotion of any sort. The morning was like many others—nothing special, just the usual oppressive Savannah summer heat. My brothers, Jason, Andy, and Peter, were there as was my mother and, of course, Greta. She was lying in the kitchen, on the floor next to the breakfast table. Andy and Peter knelt beside her, stroking her ears and neck. She turned her eyes to meet me as I walked into the room, and I felt a tinge of anger pass over me. I wanted her to look sick or desperate. Instead she flashed that familiar white smile, her ears cocked forward, and her huge pink tongue bounced in time to her lively panting. She was happy to see me. I could see the welcome in her face. Damn dog! Don't you know what is happening here?

But she didn't know. How could she? I sometimes wonder exactly how much an animal can understand of emotion. Happiness and excitement are easily recognizable. There's no question. Cocked ears, a closed mouth, furrowed brow, and that amusing tilt of the head convey curiosity plainly enough. But when it comes to more complex emotions like guilt or regret or perhaps even love or sadness, these are sentiments that

128

require a certain level of cognizance that we don't usually attribute to animals. Even beyond this comes the understanding of time. Now I know that animals experience some fashion of the past simply because they have the ability to remember people, places, and things. But is this understanding of the past (if it can be called that) coupled with any perception or concept of future events? And if so, one inevitably wonders if an animal like a dog, a Rottweiler, like Greta, can this animal have a sense of its own mortality? I'd like to think not. I'd like to think that today was another day for her, a good day.

The four brothers she had known over the last six years were all together, and that was not a common occurrence. In fact, it only happened twice a year in a good year. Her family would gather for two large meals long after the summer sun abated, and she would fill her belly with leftover turkey scraps and an occasional biscuit that she would devour in one quick, greedy gulp. (The ability to savor is one trait she definitely lacked.) The second meal was preceded or sometimes followed up with an exchange of gifts. Greta always got a new bone or something very large to chew on, which would take her absolutely no time to work through. One year she got a new red nylon collar on which was embroidered her name, Greta Smith. It was commonly referred to as her necklace, and she knew it was hers. If you removed it and held it out at arm's length, she would push her nose through the open loop and work it back around her neck. It wasn't as if she knew she was supposed to wear it. She got into that thing with the vigor of someone throwing on a favorite T-shirt or some personal item of clothing that makes them feel comfortable and more like themselves. But today was not Thanksgiving or Christmas, and the only new item meant for Greta was fifteen cc's of pink sleep brought in a plastic bag by the last stranger she would ever meet.

Several months before, we began to notice that Greta would occasionally wince from some phantom pain. I passed by her once thinking I had stepped on her foot. She whipped her head back toward her rear legs as she cried out, her eyes searching for the source of the stick. From her reaction, it must have been sudden and sharp. This began to occur with increased frequency, and she started having trouble getting up. Mom would give her aspirin hidden in a lump of peanut butter on a spoon. That seemed to take care of the pain for a while. We joked that she was making the connection and learning to put us on—whimper and you get peanut butter. She whimpered a lot, and we went through a lot of peanut butter. When she could no longer stand and aspirin wasn't enough to curb the pangs, we knew it was more than arthritis or dysplasia. Mom took her to the vet, and I got a call the next evening. Greta had cancer. The phantom pain in her legs was no apparition or learned trick to get peanut butter. She had a large tumor on her spine that was putting pressure on the nerves to her hindquarters. It could probably be removed, but she also had a spot on her lung, "a metastasis," my mother told me plainly as physicians do. Surgery was to be performed right away. Dad wanted to know the cost, and Mom already had the surgeon's name and personal information. My father would have given the thumbs up, there is no question, but he just wanted to weigh the options before making a choice and perhaps to balk at the exorbitant price of the procedure. I found this kind of amusing coming from a plastic surgeon.

I didn't see Greta for several weeks after that phone call. Mom had her put into a physical therapy program in Charleston after the surgery on her spine. It sounded kind of like a spa for dogs. Greta was getting hydro-therapy daily as well as grooming and lots of other attention. The funny thing was that Greta was taken to Charleston by the vet in his private plane. I have this vision of the two of them in an old World War I biplane, flying along the coast from Savannah to Charleston with Greta in goggles and a long flowing scarf around her neck, smiling with her tongue hanging out. That's the way she did it out the car window or on the bow of the boat in the afternoon zooming down the Vernon River. Man, that dog loved the wind in her face. Nothing like going for a ride!

For the grim procedure at hand we laid out the doggie bed and a blanket, but Greta was unable to get up from beside the kitchen table. We decided not to move her. The vet, a woman in her mid-thirties wearing cutoff sweatpants and a jersey, came to the house just after 11 A.M. Her name was Beth. Greta greeted her warmly from her position on the floor. It broke us up a little to see her get so excited at meeting this new stranger. She wanted to stand, but couldn't manage. After brief intro-ductions, we all knelt around Greta and showered her with as much love and attention as we could muster; and she soaked it up in that simple way she had about her. My wife, Alissa, had stopped by from work to see the family and give Greta her last good-bye; but she felt uneasy, as did we all, when Beth walked us through the process and told us what to expect. Just after the vet delivered a warning of preparation for a final gasp of breath marking the completion of the procedure, Alissa hugged me and slid out quietly.

At this point in time there were no real tears from anyone yet. Peter, my youngest brother who was home for the summer after his first year in college, left his crouched position and went to the far window. I couldn't see his face, but I heard him sniffle a bit and raise his hand to his brow while his gaze remained fixed out the window. My mother caught this too, and stood and approached him. I thought she was going to give him a hug, but as she turned her eyes back to mine, I saw her face twisted with grief. She changed her course and stood off to the side, alone and facing away. That's when it hit me. I felt my throat knot and my eyes begin to well with tears. I knew why my dad had chosen to stay at work. It is much easier to keep it together when you don't have to look at someone you love losing it. And this was a big family. It was all around you.

My hands never left Greta. I pressed her velvety black ears through my hands and brought my focus back to her sweet face. A tear rolled down my nose and dropped onto the rug beside her head, but I don't think she noticed. Andy was at her back running his hands down her neck to the thick fur on her shoulders and speaking softly to her. Of all the brothers, I think Andy had the deepest connection with Greta. My oldest brother, Jason, sat on his knees and looked over the scene not seeming to know what to make of it.

Beth removed the contents of her plastic bag. She had two syringes full of a pink liquid and a large folded plastic bag much like the ones you put your leaves in

132

only thicker gauge. She asked us to hold Greta. The smaller needle was uncovered, and she told us that it was a mild sedative to let Greta relax. I felt my nose begin to close up. Andy and I held Greta tightly but affectionately about her head as Beth pulled the loose skin on her shoulders together and administered the first shot. It passed almost unnoticed except for a short reflexive jerk and a low growl as she removed the needle. Beth moved away quietly and the family came back in.

Almost twenty minutes passed, or at least it seemed that way. There was some question as to whether the sedative would have any effect on our big girl, but the muscles that once pushed Greta to around one hundred pounds had withered significantly and you could see the twisted spine and bony pelvis of our proud dog. She must now have been only about seventy-five pounds or less, and the sedative began to show signs of taking hold. Her head lay on the rug and her eyes began to roll a little. The distinctive panting slowed to smaller, quick breaths, and at one point her breathing became so faint that I wondered if she had expired from the first shot. It was time, and you could see the reality of the situation weighing on the expressions of everyone in the room.

Beth removed the cap from the large syringe, revealing a two-inch silver spike. I couldn't believe we were doing this. She lifted the front left leg and applied a tourniquet, but Greta's blood pressure was too low from the sedative and her weakened condition to find a plump vein. We all held our breath as the needle entered her leg. Greta didn't flinch or growl this time. The half-open slits of her eyes revealed only whites. Apart from the gentle sounds of suppressed mourning, the room was completely silent, yet I felt the tension build as if we were surrounded by an orchestra at the top of an earsplitting crescendo about to reach its climax. All eyes were fixed on the plunger when Beth withdrew the needle. Everyone breathed again and the room was still once more. She probed several more times, each push bringing back the roar of the music and the lack of breath; and each time the small circle of observers labored with the grief struggling to break free. It was exhausting. She moved onto the right leg and finally to the withered left rear before the needle found its mark. At the head of the syringe a small cloud of crimson backed into the pink fluid, and Beth returned it to the vein with her thumb easing down on the plunger. Our stifled emotions poured forth as the barbiturate eased into Greta's limp body. Andy came down on her, his chest against her back as he sobbed. The tears streamed down my face, and snot ran from my nose in a long clear line swaying off my upper lip. I wanted to wipe it away, but I couldn't let go of my dog. No one could. All I could see were hands all over Greta, clinging to her as her life slipped quietly away. I put my hand on her nose and felt the breathing stop. It took no longer than twenty seconds. Beth leaned in with a stethoscope, pressing it to Greta's chest. "She's gone." A second wave came in.

Like many people, I have experienced losing pets. When our family lived in Durham, my first little buddy was Munchkin, a mangy Lhasa apso. The maid ran over his head in the driveway. That memory is more like a still shot, because I can remember the event, even the rug we buried him in, yet I cannot recall any of the emotion involved. About that same time I acquired Duke & Duchess, a pair of guinea pigs from the pre-school I was attending. I don't remember how they went. Along the way there have been hamsters, a pair of gerbils (whose babies were squeezed until their eyes popped out by Andy as a child), a rabbit, cats, and a huge Rottweiler named Heidi, similar in appearance to Greta except for an additional twenty pounds of solid muscle and attitude to match. I was away at college when she died, and I suppose that it was the distance that cushioned the blow that time. But this experience of losing Greta was unlike any of the others. It wasn't just because she was the sweetest, most human dog I have ever known. My relationship with her had come full circle. I was there when she was just a few weeks old, and I had just held her head as she died, six short years into her life.

I said before that I had had no notion of what to expect as I headed to the house aside from knowing that it would be difficult and I didn't want to go. When Greta passed away, the very precise moment that the spark of life left her, I realized that I was carrying around the preconceived notion that I would know by looking at her, that there would be a physical change in her appearance somehow. I had never witnessed a death so closely, and I remember numerous childhood conversations with people who told romantic versions of their experiences with expiration and how the body suddenly looked like an empty shell as the spirit departed. I wasn't looking for this to happen; I expected it as a regular course of action. In some way I needed it for comfort, a magical moment of real life passing into the supernatural, ensuring that there is something there, but it didn't happen. Had it not been for my hand at her nose searching for a breath that would never come, Greta could have been only sleeping. There was no moment and definitely no magic. She was just dead.

I sat by her side for a few moments before I began to feel silly for continuing to caress her head. I leaned to Peter and quietly suggested that we go outside and find a place to bury her. Soon after we were out the back door, Jason followed, and the three of us strolled around the backyard, wiping away the last of our tears. The first levity that was brought to our situation was from Peter. Jason and I had surveyed a place near to where I knew they had buried Heidi, and Peter speedily objected with a look of horror. We couldn't do that! I was a bit confused as Peter led us further along the bluff to the south and indicated a stretch of earth and straw under the oaks that lined the marsh. When he finally got around to offering an explanation for his insistence that we avoid the previous burial area, his mouth cracked into an uncomfortable smile and his face lightened a bit. He didn't remember exactly where Heidi was laid in the ground. He did know the general vicinity, but there were other bodies there as well, the cats Kita and Oreo, and he didn't want to happen upon their bodies or whatever was . . . He couldn't finish the sentence, and we all laughed a subdued sort of laugh at his revulsion to the thought of uncovering what lay in the ground . . . somewhere. It was okay to laugh, wasn't it? Soon we chuckled wholeheartedly and all felt a little bit better. The smiles and sounds of happiness were very welcome, and Andy warmed quickly as he joined us.

We borrowed a couple of shovels from the neighbors

and decided on a spot in the shade for the grave. The four of us agreed that the hole should be four feet deep (we had forgotten that the heat index was well over a hundred degrees) and with enough room to lay Greta out with her head facing the river, a beautiful view that looks due east into the morning sun. (It is very strange the way we handle death, not the dying, but the duties following, the careful attention to every detail in consideration of the deceased.) With the specs all completed, I began the digging. Jason joined in for a dozen or so scoops of dirt before he relinquished his shovel to Andy. He had worked the eleven-to-seven shift at the hospital the night before, and I could see that it was beginning to take its toll; but he never complained. Andy resumed the digging, and we sent Peter away to get a hatchet for all of the roots we were encountering. Don't ask me how this happened, but when Peter returned, wielding the mini-ax that my dad kept so sharp you could almost shave with it, Andy broke into his own impression of Joe Pesce digging Spider's grave in the movie *Goodfellas*. We were cracking up at his mafioso performance, and that's pretty much how it went as we dug. We kept things light. It was cathartic in a way. The energy of each brother's comedic attempts directly corresponded to the amount of anguish he had released in the kitchen.

I am glad I didn't notice this at the time, because it would have screwed up experiencing it; but something was happening there in the afternoon sun that had not occurred in years. We were all working together. We didn't talk about anything of any importance like what was going on in our lives or some crazy difference of opinion we carried. We traded off the shovels and sweat like swine as the pile of dirt went from black to reddish-brown to a lighter more sandy-textured earth, and we just worked. In fact, I think I can say that we enjoyed ourselves. And we enjoyed each other, equally. I felt a sense of connection to my brothers that I hadn't felt in years. Put four boys in a family and space them with thirteen years between the first and the last and you are going to have issues. Every family has them. The older you get and the more you settle into your life, develop a family of your own and spend more and more time away, the more issues and differences you get. But for one brief hour as we dug a grave for a dog that we all loved in our own way, it was like we were kids again—that time in your life when you are naively unspoiled by experience. We were happy to be together and it felt right—effortless.

We reached the proper dimensions and depth of the hole in just under an hour. Unlike Andy, I had kept my shirt on and I was completely soaked in sweat. The seventy-degree air of the house chilled the skin under my drenched clothes as we entered through the back door. Peter had gone back into the house sometime while we were digging and had arranged Greta's body on the floor, making her appear as if she were snoozing comfortably at the foot of the table. We almost tiptoed in, careful not to wake her. I knelt down and felt her head. She had stiffened up a little and had lost the warmth that we take for granted when touching a living creature. You forget how much heat we put out when blood courses through our veins, but it is so damned obvious, the lack of heat, when the life force is gone. She really appeared to be sleeping . . . except for one thing. Her tongue hung out of her mouth like that of every prize animal I have ever seen that has fallen victim to a hunter's careful and deadly aim. I tilted her head and tried to tuck the cold pale tongue back into her mouth, but it wouldn't stay. There were tears this time, but the sting of the loss had dulled a bit as we went about our work. Andy unfolded the heavy plastic bag and slid it under Greta's rear end as I lifted her back. Her body had relaxed completely, and we could smell the urine, one last dignity stolen from our girl. We got the bag around her to the neck, and Andy pulled her up into his arms almost jealously as I tried to assist. I grimaced and felt a surge of new tears to my eyes as her head swung limply over his arm, the tongue dangling. I moved to support it, but Andy was headed for the door before I could help her.

At the graveside Greta was placed on the edge of the hole. We stood for a moment looking at her head protruding from the black bag, and Andy asked if anyone wanted to say anything. I said that she was a good dog, and I heard a mumbled "Good-bye, Greta" from one of my brothers. Andy covered her head carefully, and we gently lowered her to the bottom of the hole. We straightened her legs through the bag and made sure that she was in her familiar sleeping position on her side, legs outstretched and her head flat. I remembered the feeling that I got at my grandmother's funeral when they closed the casket, the realization that I would never see her again. "Wait. I want to look at her one last time," I said. I leaned into the hole and pushed the plastic away. In that one moment I tried to soak her up, to pull in every last detail of her face. When I moved to cover her for the last time, Andy stopped my hand and sprinkled her face with a handful of moist, sandy earth.

It stood out on her clean black-and-tan fur, unnatural in a weird way. Some of the dirt fell into her open eye. I almost expected her to blink or recoil, but she didn't seem to mind. As Andy tucked the plastic around the edge of her head, it became a hard reality that she was gone. Andy let go a muffled sob as I dropped the first shovel full of earth onto the bag with a deep thud. What took almost an hour to remove, we replaced in less than five minutes. And we cried our last quiet tears.

As we packed the last of the dirt into a slightly raised mound, our spirits returned. We had all stopped crying and the process seemed complete. A family had come together to say good-bye and endure the entire circle together. It was as it should have been. We stood again, the four of us—Jason and Andy on one side, and Peter and myself on the other. I heard a slight rustle behind me, and then a very distinctive noise getting closer. It had been months since I had seen the little demon get out. Our neighbors, from whom we had borrowed the shovels, had this little Australian sheepdog that stood about knee-high with gray-and-white tufts of fur and jewel-like eyes, two distinctly different colored hemispheres, blue and white I think, surrounding the tiny black pupils. Everyone loved it when it was a pup, but it had grown into a complete terror as it moved into adulthood. It wasn't mean. It was just spastic. He would run from all the way across the yard and crash into your legs at mach six and then jump all over you (if you weren't already on the ground). I could hear him breathing right behind me, and I was angry as hell and ready to put a foot in his ass for breaking up the moment. I didn't want him running over and trying to dig at the grave. When I turned around, I expected to see him at my feet. Peter turned also. I knew he heard the little bastard too. But there was nothing there . . . except for the panting! It was all around me. I could hear it like he was at my feet, but the only dog at my feet, or four feet below, was Greta. She couldn't be the source. Peter looked at me. "Do you hear that?" I asked, not sure of what I would say if he said no. "Panting?" he exclaimed with a look of bewilderment. And then it stopped. We searched for the sound, looking in all directions. Jason and Andy hadn't heard a thing. I asked him again, and he confirmed exactly what I had heard and at the same distance. What could it have been? Someone suggested a bird in the marsh, but it had been too close and too distinct. I might not have said anything, but there were two of us who heard the same sound. It *was* something. We quickly put the thought away and turned back to the grave, dismissing the lively, excited panting as something else that just sounded like a dog. "Maybe it was Greta letting us know she is on her way to doggie heaven," I quipped. Neither Peter nor I wanted to give it much credence or make a big deal out of it. I couldn't know exactly what he heard, and I didn't want him to think I was nuts, so I dropped it and he did the same. We decided to go inside and order a pizza.

We sat around the table waiting for the pizza to come, and not a word was spoken about Greta or what had taken place here this morning. It was like a regular day again. Andy ended up taking Jason home to get some sleep, and Peter left to help the vet, whose car had broken down not far from the house. By the time the pizza came, Peter and Andy had returned and we sat together and drank cold cokes and stuffed our faces. I don't recall who brought it up, but suddenly we were discussing how good we all felt. None of us had any detectable sadness hanging around. We began speaking about Greta freely and exchanged a few funny stories about her life with us. It was incredible. I felt almost like you do leaving the gym after a good workout and a hot shower. I couldn't stop smiling.

Almost two weeks have passed since Greta left. I wanted to recount the experience, because so many things stood out in my mind as it happened, things I don't want to forget. It's always the little details, like icing on a cake, that give your life its particular flavor. They are simple to enjoy and the easiest to slide away from memory as time passes and new details roll in. Except for a few moments recounting this experience, I have shed no tears since losing her. But I don't really feel loss. I get a warm feeling inside when I think about Greta and that last day. It is a feeling of inspiration. Life seems to be at its fullest when we face emotional extremes. They let us know we are alive. I find it all too easy to slip into a mundane world, going through the motions, analyzing, calculating, and controlling. But we really control very little in this life. Things can turn on a dime, and sometimes the best place to be is honest experience and pure emotion. It's when we discover who and what we are. Fear, anger, hurt, joy, and love, experienced at a level we can't control, like being washed about on the waves of a high sea. These are the moments that shape our lives, when we endure what should not be avoided or forgotten. They are also the moments that leave us emotionally naked to those around us, and perhaps that is why we learn to avoid them with such desperation.

I will not forget Greta, and I will not be saddened with her loss. That's just the way it works here. One thing of which I am certain, everything we love we will lose, at least on this earth. But we gained the experience of her. All of the wonderful times only magnified the pain of her premature departure, yet even the pain was good. It brought four brothers together. I hadn't noticed before, but I was growing a little numb until that afternoon, perhaps a bit jaded. Like most people, I was slipping into that adult world where everything has to be explained and contained. It's all about maintaining control. As children, we react to whatever emotion takes us at the moment. I remember afternoons in the summertime with my brothers, sitting around sipping sodas and laughing so hard that the fizzy refreshment would come spewing forth from someone's nose. We would lose control and laugh until our sides hurt. When it was time for tears, they would come pouring down like a rainstorm. It wasn't embarrassing; it was just honest experience and pure emotion. As we get older, we seem to forget that, or rather, we learn to control it, and it fades slowly with our youth. It was easier to enjoy things too, back then. Of course there was magic in even the simplest of things, like when my dad used to kiss us good-night. Sometimes now it feels awkward just getting a hug from the man. I remember a time when it wasn't so difficult to say "I love you." I miss it. But somehow, through all of the hardship of that day, Greta gave it back to me for a moment. We rode the wave together, my brothers and I, our souls bared as we labored in the heat. I don't know if they felt it. Maybe it was just me. I am going to try to remember that moment, the magic of her breath all around me as she lay four feet beneath us. It was easier to believe then than it is now, not two weeks later, but I am going to try. I want to believe in magic, I want to believe in love. I *am* going to try.

STEPHEN M. SMITH

HANNAH
HARPER

Hannah had been lost. I caught a glimpse of the little brown dog staggering down the center of a major roadway. Like a frantic traffic cop, I jumped out in the street to stop the oncoming cars from what seemed to be every angle; she ran to me. She was homeless, dirty, and sick, her body infested with fleas and ticks. I brought her home and no one ever claimed her.

Hannah received immediate medical attention that required surgery. It was after a series of long hot baths that the grease on her body began to dissolve, revealing a beautiful blonde coat. It is surprising how fostering a living being can have such a reverse affect on people. When I found Hannah, there was never a time that I, myself, had felt so lost. It was the aftermath of September 11th and most of my life; the World Trade Center had been my playground. I remember going to work with my father as a little girl riding up and down the elevators from the concourse to the obervation deck and back. Oh how my ears would pop.

My dad was the director of operations for the towers and had worked there since the demolition of the preexisting neighborhood. He retired in 1997. In a funny way those buildings were like part of our family.

I sat on the conference-room floor at my job in Savannah and watched the towers tumble down. Where are my brothers? I thought. I tried to call my mother; the phone lines were down. Both of my brothers—Jimmy, a fireman, and Richie, a policeman—worked in Manhattan. I thought of the hundreds of people I knew who could be in that building or on the streets below at that particular time. I remembered my friend, Michael Hannan; his office was toward the top.

It was late in the day when I found out that my family was safe, but they hardly walked away unscathed. Among the many missing that we had known, nine firemen from my brother's firehouse never made it back. There were friends young and old who perished in the building that day. It was all so cruel. From that day on, the world had changed and we would never be the same. Michael Hannan never made it home that night.

It was a Friday afternoon in Savannah. Time had gone by since that horrific day, but not much had changed in my mind. It was raining outside; but that didn't matter, every day was cloudy to me. I remembered that it was Mrs. Hannan's sixtieth birthday and that I had forgotten to send her the card I had picked up. The little dog in the road interrupted the thought. It was the same dog that would soon reveal the same hair color as that of Mrs. Hannan's son and be named in his memory.

Now, when I walk out the door each night with the memory of a departed old friend, I also have a new friend walking on her leash, by my side. Although there is still so much pain to endure and so many questions that will never be answered, I am comforted by her presence and I can tell that she is grateful for mine.

JANE HARPER

DEIMOS ("MAMA'S GIRL")

Three years ago my doctor told me that I had to sell my horse. I had been competing in dressage for years, and now, just like that, it came to an end. My doctor said, "You can either walk or ride, but not both. If you continue horseback riding, the degeneration in your knees will progress at an alarming rate." So I sold Chase and my heart broke. Not many people know the truth, but a horse takes up a lot of room in your heart.

My husband, Dave, and I talked about getting a couple of dogs to show, to try and fill that void. We tried for years to agree on what breed of dog. I liked shepherds and Dobermans; he liked Labs and goldens. We looked, talked, and researched. No luck. We couldn't agree.

In 2001 we went to Ohio to visit Dave's sister, Amy, and her family, who happened to have two Great Dane pups. Oh, they were adorable. "I love Great Danes," I said. "I had a friend in school who had two, and they were the greatest dogs, so smart and friendly."

Dave was shocked. "You like Great Danes? I never asked you because I just figured you wouldn't like them. I love Great Danes too." So finally we had agreed on a breed of dog.

Considering that Amy had done research on her breeder, we decided to check out the litter. Dave and I decided we wanted two pups, as Great Danes are very social animals. We drove out to the breeder's, and the litter was out playing in the side yard. That's when I saw "my girl"—a beautiful, chubby, little girl with a cold. So I lay down on the ground and sat her on my chest, and she looked at me with those special little eyes—one brown, and the other, three-quarters brown and one-quarter blue. I had found my girl. Dave fell in love with a little white runt with blue eyes and barely any spots. We canceled our flight, rented a mini-van, and drove home with our new babies.

My little girl became Deimos (Latin for "panic"), and the white runt became Phobos, who opted to write his own story [see pages 151–52]. As they grew, Phobos stole the limelight. Everyone just loves the great white Dane with the blue eyes, and Deimos was left in the shadows. Although she was everyone else's second favorite, she was my first.

Deimos has always been the "good kid" of the family, though she does like to shred paper when given the opportunity. She never whines. She listens well and just loves attention. She's been in off-lead obedience training since she was four months old, and demonstrates her faithfulness daily. People ask me all the time if Dave and I will have kids. I just smile and tell them we already have.

Deimos is my "beautiful girl." She is a true harlequin, white with black patches over her head and body, but not her neck. She's shorter than Phobos, but still a good three inches taller than your average Rottweiler or Akita. She loves baby carrots and ice cubes, and just

149

hanging around with her mama. It figures that a dog the size of a horse could fill the void left by one. I miss my Chase, but I love my Deimos.

KIMBER MYERS

PHOBOS ("COW," "GREAT-WHITE HOPE")

I find myself a bit confused about my identity. You see, my sister, Deimos [see pages 148–50], and I are harlequin Great Danes, though my mama calls us cows. And she named us after moons, the moons of Mars to be exact. I don't know much about moons, other than that they probably won't fit in my mouth. You would be surprised, though, what does fit. Mama says my name means "fear" in Latin, though the only thing you have to fear of me is my drool. I can sling my drool yards, or wrap it around my snout, depending on my mood.

I live with Mama and Da, as well as my real sister, two half-sisters, and two half-brothers. I love all my brothers and sisters, even if the kitties don't appreciate my drool. Gabriel and Frazier usually just bat me on the nose and growl. The ferrets are much more fun to play with. They don't even mind if I put them in my mouth. I told you you would be surprised what would fit.

Despite my lack of spots and ice-blue eyes, I am not an albino, and I am not deaf. I do, however, have selective hearing. And even though some people say I look dopey, I am actually very smart. I understand English, German, and sign language. I am even teaching Mama

151

and Da to understand "dog," although they are a little slow on the uptake.

One of my favorite things to do is to go to Forsyth Park and play with all of my friends. After that, we sometimes go to Malone's and listen to the band, though they never play enough Jimmy Buffett. Every weekend we go downtown. Sometimes we walk along River Street, City Market, and sometimes just around the squares. If we stay at home, I love to play in the water; Deimos and I have our own pool. I also love to wrestle with my Da. He's a big guy, six feet tall, but I'm taller if I stand on my back legs.

Mama says that we're "well traveled," whatever that means. But if it has anything to do with all those hotels we get to visit, or with the elevators we get to ride in, I love it. The best part of staying at hotels is that I get to jump in the shower with Da. I can tell that he loves it too, because he always yells in excitement. Sometimes, if I really surprise him, he calls me a "stupid dog" or an "idiot," which must be a great compliment, considering how excited he is when he yells it. Even if we don't stay in a hotel, Deimos and I love to go for rides in the car, though Deimos always calls shotgun.

Remember, the next time you are driving through downtown Savannah and see two really big black-and-white dogs, it's probably Deimos and I. Please come over and say "Hi." I love every opportunity to slime a new friend. And if you have a dog of your own, bring 'em. We love to make new dog friends, too.

PHOBOS

TIPPY GORDON

Hello. My Gordon family mom, Ms. B., rescued me from the Tallahassee Animal Shelter in 1989. 1 was in this huge kennel that had "Vicious! May bite!" written on my door. Now, who in their right mind could be afraid of a three-pound poodle? Luckily not my mom. I was just old and cranky. I was about eight years of age in 1989, so that makes me, let's just say, older and much crankier now.

Not to worry. I really lucked out with my family. I'm one of about thirty-eight rescued special-needs animals at the Gordon zoo. I'm still top dog though, so it's okay. The only ones close to me on the list are the old cats, Scooter and Cinder Kitty. Since they tend to stay on their side of the house, I tolerate them.

Early mornings, Ms. B. and I try to sneak out onto the screened porch for her coffee and my milkbone. If we're lucky, we'll have some quality time before the barnyard wakes. Oops, we didn't hide well this morning. "Hee Haw!" Yep, Jethro saw us. He's the miniature donkey who blisters in the sun. He lives in the pasture with "Naaa! Naaa! Naaa!" Gerty the Grungy Goat, Penny Goat, and Prissy Goat. They make the most noise, but sometimes—oh, no—"Oink, Oink" Petunia, the big abandoned pot-bellied pig, will chime in. The horses (we have three and a pony) stay pretty calm until feeding actually starts. Okay, Ms. B., you get up to feed them so they'll hush. I'll finish my bone.

"Woof, Woof." Here they come, barking as usual. The four big dogs are out to play. They aren't so bad. After all, they are outside. Oh, what's that I hear coming down the stairs? Well, so much for my peace and quiet. Ms. B's little girl, Kenerly, and her epileptic Pekingese, Ting, are up. What a hyper little dog that Ting is. At least she keeps the six-year-old child happy . . . and away from me.

Well, Mom, you might as well take off the cage covers and let those parakeets start chirping too. Oh, and that one, Lucky Bird. Why did you ever teach him how to talk? Okay, that's good. Let Pretty Girl bunny on the back porch to thump around while I'm trying to eat. Good thing the other ten bunnies are outside. And, at least it is not nighttime. Those handicapped flying squirrels would be out making noise too . . . all on the porch . . . peeping like little birds. Plus, there's that hamster on his wheel. Doesn't he get it by now? He's not going anywhere!

Yum. Good bone. Oh, hi Dad. You're up. Guess what that means . . . "Bark. Bark!" Ms. B, where are you? Come and get me. "Bark." Oh, here she comes. Yeah, I know, time for my heart medicine. Now, take me potty again, then upstairs for my nap. Ah, that's it. Got the bed all to myself with my blankie, extra milkbones, bowl of fresh water, and my pillow slide—just in case I gotta get down.

You know, we have a lot of special animals here at the Gordon zoo. I think I speak for all when I say, "Ain't life grand." Especially as long as I'm top dog.

TIPPY

CID

I adopted Cid, a retriever-Lab mix, when he was six weeks old. His mother tragically hemorrhaged and died while delivering him and his eleven brothers and sisters. He has been very special to me since day one and was a very good puppy. A perfect little guy from birth, Cid only cried when he was hungry or needed to go outside. This made sleeping quite easy for me, since I am a schoolteacher and get up very early.

When Cid was four months old, I recognized that he had a problem. Cid was having difficulty walking properly. I took him to Dr. Bremer, and we discovered that Cid had severe hip dysplasia. His hip sockets had deteriorated to the point that he barely had any sockets left. I listened to my options and immediately decided that he was too wonderful to be put down and scheduled him to have his hip fixed. Dr. Bremer consulted Dr. Case, who did the procedure on Cid. We were all amazed at how quickly Cid recovered, and five months later they fixed his left hip. Two new hips before he was one year old! Cid's rehabilitation was easy and fun. We walked for miles and ran even more. I gave Cid massages, and we regularly busted into the apartment pool after hours for a therapeutic swim three times a week. He now shows little sign of his hip trauma. He runs with the best of them and nothing slows him down.

Cid now lives with Mark, my husband; Desi, his canine sister [see pages 158–59]; and me. We are a happy family of four, and although Cid is bigger than Desi, he lets her rule the roost. They spend their days in our large backyard, running, playing, and waiting for Mommy and Daddy to get home. Cid will pace in front on the sliding glass door to come in and have treats, then pace to go back outside to run with the squirrels. Cid and Desi sleep side by side on their puffy feather beds and are the best of friends.

I would like to share with you the list of Cid's Top Ten favorite things to do in Savannah: (1) sneak down the hall, a no-no, to see me in the bathroom and try to steal a drink from the bathtub faucet; (2) look out the storm door at his friends in the neighborhood to bark a friendly hello to them; (3) go for a walk at 6:00 A.M. with Desi through our Wilmington Island neighborhood; (4) go to the Bremer Veterinary Clinic, where they spoil him rotten; (5) go in and out of the sliding glass door to the backyard (he'll wear himself out doing this); (6) have a bath; (7) chase tennis balls at the landfill, a.k.a. Charles C. Brooks Field; (8) chase the squirrels in Forsyth Park; (9) drool water from his bowl in the kitchen through the family room (without even knowing it); and (10) ride in Daddy's yellow 1973 VW Beetle to Tybee Island and back while breathing in the fresh salty air.

KAREN W. BEST

157

DESI

Hi! I am an American Staffordshire terrier. My mom's friend, Melanie, helped her name me, after Jimmy Buffet's Desdemona. I had a very rough start in life. Give me a few minutes and I'll tell you all about it. I was discovered in 1997 in, of all places, the trunk of a car. Boy, was I ever in a dilemma. The car was just about to be compacted, so I yelled as loud as I could, and thank goodness, I was heard. The nice people at PALS took me over to PETsMART, where much to my joy my new mom was waiting to adopt me.

I was still a little nervous, what with the close call in that other car, so when my mom put me in her car, I insisted that I sit on her lap. I shivered and whined all the way to our home on Wilmington Island, where my new canine brother, Cid [see pages 156–57], was anxious to meet me. My nervousness went away almost immediately the minute I walked into my new house. Loving my new surroundings, I strutted my stuff. I decided that since Cid was almost twice my size, I better let him know that I planned to be boss. It worked and I have been queen bee ever since.

Things were going very well for me until that dark

day in 1999. You see, I tore my ACL and this was quite a terrible ordeal. Fortunately Dr. Chara was able to fix me up. She had fishing twine—yes, the kind you find in your tackle box—sterilized for me at the vet school in Charleston. Dr. Chara sewed me up with this fishing line at the Bremer Veterinary Clinic, and I haven't missed a hop, skip, or a jump since. I love the humans in my life and especially the attention they give me. My favorite trick is to flop on my back for a belly rub, followed by my lick of your toes to say "thank you." Although I'm not crazy about getting my bath, I do tolerate one to be rewarded with that wonderful brushing from my mom and dad. I sleep by my brother, Cid, and he and I have a wonderful relationship. My hair is shorter than his, and in the cooler months I insist that my parents cover me with a towel to keep me warm. I am amazingly still all night and keep my towel around me until I go outside in the morning. My mom says that this is important because if I get cold I'll wake up the whole house with my snoring.

I have a very happy life in Savannah and I'm a bundle of energy. I am always by our sliding glass door, waiting for snack time. When the door is opened, I spin my feet on the hardwood floor, just like you see in the cartoons, gaining traction to be first to reach the kitchen. I always beat Cid to our bowls, and I get to be the first to check for a snack or a morsel that someone has left for me.

DESI

159

LADY OF
SAVANNAH
("SAVANNAH")

Okay. I admit it. I was unsure of my future at first when Holmes, my master, took me from my mother and brought me home to live in a farmhouse with a bunch of fraternity boys. Holmes, who was a junior at Hampden-Sydney College, missed his family dog so much that he decided to adopt me from a nearby farm and name me for his beloved town, Savannah. (Between you and me, I think he also was hoping a puppy would help him attract more attention from those pretty Sweet Briar and Hollins girls.)

Boy, was I wrong to be worried. My master proved early on that he was as devoted to me as I to him. Never one to leave me at home, he took me wherever he went—from college classrooms to hunting fields to football tailgates. I became his sidekick, his sure companion. And there I've stayed for more than a decade, and through all of the adventures.

After college I became a city dog as Holmes brought me home to Savannah and bought us a beautiful, but neglected, row house on Jones Street in the historic downtown area. The first time I saw it, I remember

160

thinking that the farmhouse looked like the Ritz compared to this. I mean, you could see the sky from the ground floor of the three-story house. But once again Holmes proved that my worries were needless.

Most nights for almost a year Holmes would come home from working all day at the Hussey, Gay, Bell, and DeYoung engineering firm, and together we would work into the late hours to restore the home to its original beauty. Oh, the excitement I felt after we finally moved in. My tail wouldn't stop wagging for a week straight. From the first days, my favorite thing to do in the house has been to sit in the bay window on the parlor floor and watch all of the activity on Jones Street, from SCAD students to horse-and-carriage tours.

With the restoration complete, Holmes and I were ready to sit back and relax for a while. We tried . . . we really did. But something just wasn't right. We both agreed that something was missing from our lives. That something was a young woman for us to love. So Holmes searched high and low and finally found for us the perfect one, living just south of here on St. Simons Island. From the moment we met, Lisa and I have had a special bond. Maybe it's because we're both blondes. Or maybe it's because she rubs my belly and calls me Pooh Bear. Regardless, I was thrilled when our team of two grew to three when Holmes married Lisa.

A couple years later, we grew to four as Holmes and Lisa gave me a companion, Hampton, a black Lab puppy. Full of endless energy, he's taught me how to be a puppy again—at least in mind and spirit, if not body. And I've taught him how to sit, fetch, dig, and get into the garbage. It's a fair trade-off.

Lately though, my time has been occupied with the

161

most recent addition to our family, a precious baby boy named Gus. Just learning how to crawl, he loves to come over and climb all over me. Thank goodness, with age comes patience. That and gray hair. Oh well, at least Holmes is getting some gray too. As always, we do it together.

SAVANNAH

LACEY

I'm pretty new to Savannah. My family drove to Raleigh a few months ago to get me, and I have to tell you that it was love at first sight when I met them.

Seems my sister, Chloe, had her heart set on finding a blue merle collie, and I was holding out for a ten-year-old girl who lived in a neighborhood full of kids and other dogs. We each got exactly what we were looking for, and I love my life.

I love Savannah, too. Being a house dog is wonderful; but we also have a big, open space next to a lagoon nearby, and there are lots of animals, girls on bikes, boys playing basketball, and moms and dads walking and jogging around our circle. So I have plenty of things to bark at. I like going to Forsyth Park, but my most favorite thing to do is run around the old Islands YMCA field when the kids are practicing baseball and soccer. Actually I think my most favorite thing is trying to catch the ducks that hang around our lagoon. No, you know what, now that I think about it, my most favorite thing to do is just hang out with Chloe and my dad.

I have a brother. He's a kitty named Rainbow, a very

163

ornery-looking Persian who thinks he's a big shot. It didn't take me long to figure out that he's okay for a cat, and we've been pals pretty much right from the start.

The little guy—that's what we all call him—teases me a lot because he knows I'll get excited. Nobody likes to play more than I do, and he and I will tear through the house with me after him. Mom loves that. I'll chase him under the beds, behind furniture, and up on the counters. When he lets me catch him, I hold him on the floor in my mouth while he punches my nose with his front paws. He's pretty tough, and it's fun when he's around to play during the day when nobody else is home. The only thing that I wish he'd do with me is tug on my torn up, slobbery, old white sock the way my dad does. I can't get him to do that, no matter how hard I try.

I don't completely understand it, but people say the nicest things about my coloring. I've been out walking with my dad, and people will stop their cars to say how pretty I look. I enjoy the attention, and we always thank them, but there were lots of blue merles where I came from, so I don't see what the big deal is.

I suppose I'm just a little unusual. Dad told me he saw a beautiful blue merle shelty downtown near Clary's one day, and we met two very friendly blue merle Australian shepherds at the Doggie Festival. I guess there just aren't very many collies in Savannah. I don't know why—they'd love it here as much as I do.

LACEY

PRECIOUS MAGNOLIA ("MAGGIE," "MINNIE ME")

I am a Shih Tzu and my name is Maggie. Actually my Aunt Kathy named me Precious Magnolia, but since I weigh only ten pounds my name is bigger than I am. Now my friends know me as Maggie, or more often, Minnie Me. I came to live in Savannah in 1998, when I was only eight weeks old. I flew in on an airplane from Missouri and was so small that a lady at the airport asked if I was a guinea pig. I was a ball of fur and so happy to be in Savannah. I moved in with my human mom, Michelle, and my canine sister, Molly.

Life was not easy for me, at first. When I was only a few months old, Dr. Lester found that I had hip dysplasia. He fixed my leg, and during my stay I became great friends with all the staff at the Island Veterinary Clinic. Soon after, I had an accident and got a chemical burn in my eye. Dr. Lester saved my eye and I can see shadows now. My other eye is perfect, so I have no problems seeing in my little world.

After a few more traumas, my life started going really great. We live in a house on Wilmington Island, where I like to sit in the front window to watch all the action on my street. I am a very smart girl. I know most of my toys by name and will find them and bring them to you when you ask me. I like to play fetch, and my favorite toy is my pocketbook. My mom puts treats in my purse, and I work diligently with the zipper until I open it and eat my treats.

We go for walks every afternoon in my neighborhood, and I've made many friends along the way. Since I am quite social, my mom takes me every place that the owners will let me in. My favorite place is City Market, and I try to get there every weekend. The humans at Vinnie Van Go-Go's are especially nice to me, and I like to go there on Sunday afternoons. They give me water, and I sit on my mom's lap and eat calzones. I like to watch the tourists, and they often stop and talk to me. I enjoy the parks and walking in the squares downtown. I have been to the Blessing of the Pets and, most recently, to the Doggie Carnival in Daffin Park. I like to ride in the car and often go to Tybee for strolls in the afternoons.

I lost my sister, Molly, to cancer in April. I was very close to her and miss her very much. I am going through a lot of changes; it's just me and my mom now, but we have a happy life. I love my life in Savannah, and I am proud of my true Savannah name, Magnolia. I look forward to my next trip from the island—seeing my pals, enjoying all the charms of the city, and walking downtown among the Magnolia trees.

MAGGIE

166

HANNAH ("THE HAN," "HAN HAN")

Bark, bark, bark, bark, bark, bark, bark, bark, bark, bark, bark, bark, bark, bark, bark! Pardon me, but this is how I always greet a new acquaintance. Since I am a miniature schnauzer, I am predisposed to be somewhat "yappy," as my parents call it. But I do think that they have comfort in knowing that no intruder would enter our home without my knowing about it and telling the whole world. In fact I did our neighbors a great favor when they were keeping us while our parents went on a trip. Their alarm kept going off. I think it had something to do with some high-pitched sounds in their house like a dog barking. Oh well, the second time it went off, a man entered their house and I courageously bit him on the toe of his shoe. I don't know why he had on a badge and a blue cap that looked kind of like a policeman's. And for some reason I heard my parents laughing at their dog who now had a criminal police record. They must have been confused, since I was the one that nabbed the "criminal." Otherwise, I have always been content to chase cats, squirrels, and birds, preferably in that order. Since I am now over thirteen years old, I have to admit I have slowed down

167

a bit. Not that I still don't welcome a passerby to bark at or an occasional cat to chase, but I am content to be a little more laid-back and relaxed about life these days. Also in my younger days, I was quite an energetic comic. My antics have included jumping up in trees, getting on top of the kitchen table to take a nap, and somehow getting on the kitchen counter tops to consume mass quantities of vitamins (my parents still can't figure how I managed that one, so it is my forever secret.) After these numerous incidents, my parents would give me the ultimate insult by saying I must have thought I was a feline. Yuk!

My parents and I first moved to Savannah in the spring of 1998. It was on one of these lovely spring afternoons that we went to Forsyth Park and had the good fortune of running into the editor of this book, Minnie M. Beil [see *Savannah Dogs*, pages 352–54]. Since I was a newcomer, she welcomed me with her very gracious Savannah hospitality and then introduced me to her canine playmates. It didn't matter to me that all of Minnie's friends towered over me, with my stature being just below their kneecaps. It has always been my dream to run free with the "big dogs." I must say that Minnie's friends were somewhat rude—when I nipped at their heels, they pretended not to notice. Certainly this was a pretense, however, because I have no doubt that these large animals were scared half to death. I am sure that is why all the people watching on the sidelines were laughing so hard because they could see just how frightened these gigantic monsters were of my brave self. Nothing like having a dream and it coming true.

Just after moving to Savannah, I faced my most difficult challenge—I lost my eleven-year position as the baby in the family. Suddenly all the attention was being lavished on this funny-looking, two-legged creature. At first I wasn't sure what to do, and I seriously considered chasing it up a tree like a squirrel. But now I am glad I didn't. Ethan and I are now big buddies, and I don't mind cleaning up the stray Cheerios or other goodies he drops to the floor. Not being the baby anymore isn't such a bad thing after all.

HANNAH

HAMILTON GENSER ("HAMBY," "HAMBONE," "HAMDOG")

Hi. I have had a very interesting and varied life during my twelve years. Between my mom, Naomi, and my sister, Brianne, there is an argument about my age. Mom says I am twelve, and Bri says I am eleven. As long as they keep giving me "good boy biscuits," I will be two, twenty-five, or whatever they want.

I started out on St. Simons Island, where I was thrown out in a box with two of my siblings. It seems that this little white spot on my chest was not what someone looking for a pure black Lab would want. We were left without food and water in a new subdivision called Hamilton Landing. A nice lady found us and brought us to her friends. There was an interesting little girl named Brianne. I just got out of my box and started following her. Next thing I knew, I was in the car on the way to a new home. My name, of course, came from the place where I was found.

For the first three years I would not go inside the house. Sun, rain, snow, or cold—it did not matter to me. I had plenty of interesting things to eat, like hoses, plants, small wiggly things, and landscape lighting. My mom made the lamps even tastier by putting cayenne pepper in a Vaseline sauce. I couldn't get enough. I would not eat the lights when it was cold because I could wrap myself around them to keep warm. During my formative years I also learned what "piece o' pizza" was and that it usually came in a box delivered by the "piece o' pizza" man. He would ring the doorbell and run to his car when I barked. Boy that was fun. I then learned that the mailman, UPS drivers, and Willy the Meter Man would leave when I barked, too.

In 1995 we moved to Jones Street in Savannah. This house had an interesting new game. At about the same time every day, someone came up to the front door. I would bark my meanest bark and lowest growl. Then a bunch of paper and letters came through the slot in the front door. The visitor would leave, and I had all this paper to shred. Life was good downtown. Next stop was to a house on Pulaski Square. I met the General and other friends in the square every day, and there were lots of big four-legged animals pulling carts to show who's boss. My next home was with my stepdad, Howard. What an acquisition. He has turned out to be my chef, valet, play toy, chauffeur, and anything else I can think of. It was great to be able to sit on my porch and watch the people and the dogs go by in Forsyth Park. I could also go on the back deck and toast in the sun. I noticed that next door was a cute little Lab named Minnie [see *Savannah Dogs*, pages 352–54]. She and I would stare at each other through the windows and greet each other in the park. What a "hottie."

Recently my family decided to move to the Vernon River out in the country. There are all kinds of new animals to reign over—bunnies, raccoons, squirrels, and birds. I also get to snooze in the sun in my screened-in porch (no bugs).

HAMILTON

COOKIE

I am a one and a half years old, which is too young to write my autobiography. I really should wait until I am older and have had more life experiences, but this may be my only chance to become a published author. So here is my problem: How can my memoirs be interesting when my short and happy life has been so uneventful? If I do embellish here and there, please remember I am doing it for you, the reader. My only desire is to entertain you. I think you will see as you read this that I am considerate as well as intelligent.

I'll start by telling you about my human, a boy named Richard. I am fond of all boys, but Richard is my favorite. Richard loves me and takes care of me. One of the best things about Richard is that he knows how to have fun, and we get wild together. Although Richard is pretty good at being wild, I am better. When we play chase, I run really fast. I zigzag and reverse directions so quickly that he can never catch me unless I want him to. I enjoy a game of chase combined with hide-and-seek. I am an expert seeker; no hiding place can remain undiscovered by me for long. After I find

Richard, I give him a bite (not hard of course) just to show him that dogs rule.

I am a superior athlete; I possess both speed and stamina. Sometimes Richard goes on long bike rides, and I run along with him. I am not exaggerating when I tell you that I can run for hours without tiring. I am also a good soccer player, excelling at defense. In fact, I like to catch and retrieve any type of ball or toy.

Here is another good game I enjoy playing with humans. Get them to throw your ball or toy. Run and get the object, drop it at their feet, and act like you want them to pick it up and throw it again. Just as the human is reaching for it, at the last microsecond lunge in and snatch it away in your jaws. You can usually get humans to fall for this three or four times before they get disgusted and refuse to play. If you are lucky, you might get a game of chase out of this too.

I could go on about my athletic abilities, but I must tell you about my appearance. My mother is an Australian shepherd, and my father is a Border collie. I must take after my father because I look like a Border collie. I have been told my face is pretty, but I am especially proud of my tail. The fur on it is long and thick, and I carry it curled over my back. The color of my tail is black, except for a white tip, which seems to glow in the dark when I go for walks at night with Richard and his mom.

Richard's mom says I am bossy. I don't see myself this way, but I do know what's right and the way things should be. I try to help others understand that there must be structure in our lives. Just because I sometimes like to arrange people and other dogs in a certain way doesn't mean I am obsessive or compulsive. When I go to doggie day-care, I can use my talent for directing others without causing offense to anyone, human or canine. I admit, I enjoy guiding others and helping them to see what is right, but I don't mind receiving guidance and direction myself. That is why I love obedience school. I like interacting with my humans according to well-defined rules of behavior.

I am a young dog with most of my life ahead of me. There are so many possibilities. Perhaps when I am old, I'll write a second installment of my memoirs. I should have many things to tell.

COOKIE

DAZIE-DOO ("BABY DAZIE")

It all started when I was a puppy. It was March 18, 2000. The new millennium. It was a day that would change the course of my life. This was my second week at PETsMART with my foster family. I wasn't really sure what was happening. The previous week my brother Scooby-Doo had been adopted. A lady walked over and picked me up out of the buggy. She smelled really good. "Take me home," I pleaded, "I've been waiting for you." It was suddenly all clear. My special person was here to get me. Save-A-Life had done it again. A perfect match.

Another girl held me while my new mommy filled out paperwork. This girl gave me kisses and I kissed her back. She petted me and hugged me; I liked her a lot. The little boy who fostered me tearfully said good-bye; I would miss him. I remember how he had bottle-fed me from when I was one week old and how he had taken good care of me.

When my new mommy had finished all the papers, she held me over her shoulder and walked down an aisle. I looked back at my foster parents, and remembered how I had been saved from a horrible death in a barn with my brother Scooby-Doo. Two of my brothers and sisters were frozen to death, with my real mommy.

I got a new pink collar and leash in the store, and then my new family and I went home. On the first day I met some old dogs named Bud, Lucky, and Spike. I liked them all.

I got used to the big house and yard, and I started obedience classes, where I learned to sit, stay, speak, and shake. I passed with flying colors. I got a purple collar for training; and whenever I see one of my humans holding it, I know I'm going on a walk. I love going on walks.

I'm now two and a half. My mommy and the little girl volunteer for Save-A- Life bring home foster dogs for me to play with. I teach them how to have fun, be good, and how to love again, even though I'm not always a good dog. I get to play with the kittens that they foster, too. I get sad when my friends get adopted, but I know that they went to good homes, and that Mom always will bring another friend to play with. It makes me feel happy to play with all of the dogs that she brings home because the old dogs that live with me aren't much fun. Also, I always lose weight when I play. And that's good because the vet said that I'm overweight (even though he gives me lots of treats when I see him).

So I'm living the high life here with plenty of food and love to last a million lifetimes. I would tell you bunches more, but I'm sleepy and I think I'll just take a nap.

DAZIE

177

LUCKY-DOG ("LUCKY")

This is the story of a lucky dog, born in a litter of three to my dog Budley. They came into the world in my husband's favorite recliner. Budley, raised by my cat, was somewhat surprised when she had puppies.

When Lucky-Dog was two months old, she had a little help from a five-year-old and got out of the house. Just as I realized that Lucky-Dog was out in the street, I saw a car's rear wheel run over her. A young girl had been unable to stop. She was crying, I was crying, everyone was crying. The puppy was conscious, but limp. I feared that she had broken her back. I took her inside, put her in the puppy bed, and then called my best friend to come over and examine her, as she was somewhat more knowledgeable about dogs than me. She agreed that it looked bad. We were in the other room and calling the vet when the puppy came bouncing into the room as if nothing had happened. We were stunned. My friend looked at me and said, "What a lucky dog."

During the next few weeks, my husband's patience with three puppies wore thin. We found a wonderful home for one of the pups, but still had two. Lucky-Dog always seemed to be in the doghouse. If she wasn't chewing shoes or pooping everywhere, then she was underfoot constantly. My husband finally grew impatient with her constant behavior problems and took her to the Humane Society. I was crushed. He came back home and sat down with a grim expression. He told me how he had pulled up to the front of the building, sat there with her in his lap, and looked down at her as she licked his hand. He put the truck in reverse and brought her back home. What a Lucky-Dog.

Several weeks later, and looking for help, I contacted Save-A-Life. I needed to have momma spayed and find homes for the pups. I had three small children and money was tight. Deborah Friedman had me bring momma and the pups to their mobile adoption at the Savannah Science Museum. I set out with my two oldest children, five and six, Budley, and the two pups. One of the puppies was adopted rather quickly. Not Lucky, of course. One beautiful day at home, Budley and Lucky were lying in the sun sleeping together when Mrs. Friedman came to me with a proposition. A benefactor of Save-A-Life, who had seen the two puppies together, didn't want to see them separated. She had offered to pay for Lucky's spay and shots if I would keep her. My children were thrilled. I was not. What a Lucky-Dog.

As years passed it became apparent that Lucky was not the brightest dog. She struggled to learn even the simplest of commands. When she was about six years old, the house we were renting was sold and we had to move. It was very difficult to find a rental house that would take pets. My sister lived in Atlanta on two acres of fenced-in land and offered to take Lucky. My children and Budley were heartbroken.

Two days after I returned, Lucky ran away. I was devastated. Here I was in Savannah, and Lucky was wandering around Atlanta, lost. The guilt was horrible. My sister ran ads, searched high and low, posted signs, but no Lucky. She had disappeared. Two weeks later I received a phone call. Lucky had shown up at a house about twenty miles from my sister's. The people who had found Lucky had gotten my number off Lucky's collar, but they had not secured her. By the time my sister got there, Lucky had gone. It was awful. Three weeks passed. One day when I came home, there was a message from Animal Control in a county sixty miles west of my sister's home. Animal Control had a dog with Chatham County tags that they traced to me. When I called them, I was crying so hard that it was difficult to talk. The officer told me that they had a reddish-brown dog. Was it mine? Lucky was not red. My heart sank. I said that her name was Lucky-Dog. It had to be her. The woman called her to see if she would respond. I heard her bark. It was. An elderly lady had called Animal Control because a dog was at her front door and wouldn't move. They picked her up. The night before there had been a tornado in the area. Lucky is terrified of storms to this day. The reddish color was good old Georgia clay. I went to Atlanta and brought her home to stay. What a Lucky Dog.

KATHY BRINSON

180

JUNIOR,
THE WONDER DOG
("JUNIOR")

Hello, my friends. When I was asked to write an auto-biography of my life, I was both delighted and amazed. I am an old, gentle dog, fifteen years of age. I was purchased by my owner from a dog pound for five dollars. I have often been called by my master the "five-dollar dog," among other things, depending on my owner's mood at the time or on any situations that I might have been in at the time. I am what one might call a Heinz 57 Variety; but hey, that's okay, the more variety, the better. I have the bone structure of a Lab, but the personality of a hound. Although my arthritic body does not allow me to exercise and explore much, I used to be the fastest chicken chaser in the Low Country. My owner had to move us to the vast hills of West Virginia for a brief time on account of his job requirements. What a different life from that of my be-loved Low Country.

When I was a puppy, I had to explore, and exploring I did. The neighbor had some fine-looking, plump chickens that were just beckoning to be chased. Well, chase them I did against my master's orders, but kids will be kids. As I had one of the fine, plump chickens in the clutches of my one-inch canines, I heard a loud cracking noise. I did not realize it until the next day, but I had been shot, and all for a lousy squawking West Virginia chick. (By the way, my taste for a plump West Virginia chicken has subsided greatly.)

The vet took twenty fragments out of my head, and some still remain that were unremovable. Being the tough little pup that I was, and for the love of my owner, I pulled through this chick ordeal. Since my master was a single college professor and at times required my advice, concerning both the scholarly and sometimes just the streetwise variety, I knew that he needed me.

One of my most favorite pastimes is to visit my grandparents, Royce and Jean. They let me do anything I want—sleep on the sofa,, lift my leg on any bush in the yard that I choose, howl at the moon, and even eat until I pop. What a great cook, Grandma Jean is, yum. And Grandpa Royce spoils me silly.

I also enjoy playing with my two beautiful little nieces, Jordan and Elizabeth. We play Frisbee as much as my old bones will allow; these human chicks are harder to chase than the poultry variety. Whew! At times they get out of hand and a little routy, but all I have to do is snarl at them a little and they stand at attention like little toy soldiers, and sometimes run to their mom and dad, Carrie and Neil, and tell on me. Of course I grin with my large canines and act totally innocent.

Well, I guess I'd better close for now; but as I am an old gentle dog, I've had a great life, full of people who love me, especially my dad, Benjamin, who saved me from the gas chamber and from the West Virginia chicken owner, or worse. I am a true Low Country

Gentle Dog, and even though I will leave it one day, not by choice, my heart and spirit will always roam the Low Country in search of adventure, preferably one that does not include chickens.

JUNIOR

MR. BRINKELSWORTH ("BRINKELY")
AND
MR. BAILEYKINS ("BAILEY")

Hi! I'm a young, sleek, black-and-tan, long-haired dachshund. My mommy and daddy got me when I was just four weeks old, which was almost a year ago. Although I turned out bigger than they thought, they still love me a whole lot. As a matter of fact, they just got Mr. Baileykins, my stepbrother—or as I like to think, a new toy—and me a new home with a huge yard to run and play in, where there are plenty of sticks for me to seek and destroy.

My hobbies include: eating, napping, eating, chewing on toys, napping, fetching, eating, and assisting Mr. Baileykins in total yard domination. You could say I'm the ears of the operation. Mr. Baileykins, code-named Bailey, is also a dachshund; but he is what you'd call a double-dapple shorthair. He has a white face and blue eyes. Bailey is hearing impaired, therefore I will speak on his behalf. "Brinkely is the coolest and most awesome dog in the whole wide world . . . and . . . he is my idol . . . I truly . . ." Oh, sorry about that. Anyway, Bailey was adopted when he was one year old. He had a hard life on the streets, but he doesn't really like to talk about it. Our mommy and daddy drove five hours to a veterinarian north of Atlanta in order to rescue him. Bailey only weighed six pounds when we first met, but now he's beefed up to a healthy eight pounds, which makes it harder for me to pin him down when we wrestle.

When Bailey and I first met, he didn't want anything to do with me; he was used to working solo. After a few weeks he began to see how I could help him out in his mission. Our current mission, very top secret, involves taking over the yard, then we move onto the park, and, eventually, downtown Savannah. Even if we have to do it one tree at a time, we'll get the job done. Bailey's motto is "See it, pee on it," which seems to be working well for us because we currently own half the yard and about one-fifth of Forsyth Park. Our only competition in the yard are those pesky squirrels, which we are currently trying to muscle out. They go into hiding whenever Bailey and I go out, but we know they are out there. Bailey may be deaf, but he can smell really good and spends most of his time in the yard seeking them out, while I listen for intruders. Every now and then we go on a walk with our mommy and daddy to further develop our property. That tree over there, ours . . . that bush, ours . . . that other thing over there, ours. We even own that blade of grass over there, which we are especially proud of.

Yep, it's a good life for a couple of dogs. We hang

out together a lot on the porch or we chew on our big pillow bed. We've become best buds, and I wouldn't give up this life for anything.

BRINKELY

WINSTON GOTTLIEB ("WINNIE," "WIN-MAN")

I am one of several beautiful vizslas (and one mix) that live on Jones Street. I am sure that if you passed by my house my sister Wylly [see *Savannah Dogs,* page 241–44] and I stuck our heads out the parlor floor window to greet you. Our street, especially our block, is like no other in Savannah. It is unique in the sense that our neighborhood is a family. The dogs on this block are the glue that keeps everyone happy and are appreciative of the unconditional love and friendship that exist. Some of the houses are named for people still living in them, like Mrs. Davidson, who calls my sister and me her outside pets and buys us boxes of scooby snacks. We love her the best—not because of the treats, which are yummy, but because she is a beautiful woman inside and out.

Hatcher, a springer spaniel across the street, takes his dad everywhere, even to work. Hatcher even came to my parents' church wedding. Kajah, a weimaraner, lives upstairs. She is so high energy and fun to play with. Sophie, a beautiful vizsla across the street, gives the best kisses, and when she is done with you there is no need for a bath. Her daddy hits golf balls for her to retrieve,

187

and she's a knock-out because of all her exercise. Cody, another vizsla down the street, is a stud. He's got the best yard, and we get to go over to play with him. Pete, the newest and youngest vizsla on the street, is often mistaken for me, so you know that he is one handsome pup. Dune [see *Savannah Dogs*, pages 228–33] and Bella are our pals too. We look forward to seeing them as much as we do Clarence and Leon. We hang out a lot together in Forsyth Park. Last but not least is my sister, Wylly, the squirrel hunter and my best friend.

You may be wondering why I described my friends before I begin telling you about myself. My friends and neighbors have molded me into the vizsla I am today. I am loving and kind because of those who love me.

I look out my parlor window to keep our neighborhood safe, wish tourists a big Savannah welcome, appreciate all the blessings of God, and, most importantly, patiently await my mama and daddy's arrival home. They take me out on the block to visit my friends and enjoy the city I call my home.

P.S. I want everyone to know that my daddy *picked me* out amongst many at a vizsla farm and brought me home as a Valentine's Day present for my mama. He made a promise to me that day that he would love and take care of me. Even though I got car sick and threw up on him several times on the way home, have rolled in smelly stuff that smells like skunk, chewed his favorite hats, and been a bed hog, he has always kept his promise.

WINNIE

ROXIE
IOCOVOZZI

Roxie is a two-year-old Rottweiler. When she was about two months old, I found her running down a country road in Bulloch County with a yellow rope tied around her neck. Roxie was scared, but I managed to catch her and bring her to Savannah. She quickly adjusted to her new city and family. Roxie is extremely loyal and easygoing for a Rottweiler, but she is extremely protective of her yard and home.

Recently Roxie had eight pups—seven females and one male. Seven pups survived, and Roxie proved to be a very attentive and gentle mother. Her whole world became those pups, and for five or six weeks she really thought of nothing else. Once the pups were older and able to function on their own, Roxie returned to her normal routine.

Roxie's favorite time of the day is during the evenings—curled up at my feet, with a full stomach and a secure feeling about her world. Her world could have been much different had she not been found and cared for by a special friend.

Roxie loves to go for rides in the car, especially when the destination is the river, where she can go for a swim. After her swim and run, she is ready for a nap; and if she is lucky, she can curl up in my lap and have her head stroked. She loves her dinner; and, watching her diet, I am careful to give her mostly hard food. Occasionally she'll get a few table scraps and, as a treat, a nice juicy bone.

Roxie has her own courtyard as well as a nice, spacious yard to call her own. She is very careful not to destroy plants and grass—a welcomed characteristic in larger dogs.

Roxie has had visitors from as far away as Alaska, and they all fall under her spell. By the time the visitors leave, they realize that Roxie is the real boss of the house.

Many people have the mistaken idea that all Rottweilers are bad, vicious dogs. Spending one afternoon with Roxie will dispel that thought. Although she is defensive of her home and owner, Roxie is a very loving, gentle dog—unless given a reason not to be. The environment and treatment that surrounds humans determines how they function and relate to others. If only more dogs and humans were treated with the love and attention that they naturally crave, think what a wonderful world it would be. This is the world that Roxie and I have found.

MIKE IOCOVOZZI

CHLOE

Happy Ending is what my brother calls me, but Chloe
is my real name. I am a very energetic, tricolored beagle
who does not have a clue about rabbits. You see, I prefer to search for frogs under the big oak tree in my
backyard.

I am only eighteen months old, but I have had a very
busy life. I have completed three months of obedience
school and am currently enrolled in agility classes. I
absolutely love the dog walk and jumps, and I seem to
have no fear. But the truth is I will attempt almost
anything for a treat. I have not decided how far I will
go with my formal education. Mom says I am very
affectionate and she would like for me to become a
trained therapy dog. But I am not sure what all that is
going to require. For now I am enjoying everything life
brings my way, and I will simply have to take things
one step at a time.

During the weekdays, while Mom is at work, I
spend my days lounging on the front porch of my
doghouse. When I need a better view of the neighborhood, I often climb on top of my house to check things
out. In the evenings I enjoy curling up on the couch

with a good chew bone and staring at the television. I really look forward to my weekend walks along the marsh, sniffing the tall grasses and playing with the little fiddler crabs. I have no idea what I would do if I ever caught one of those little creatures. Mom says I am a very bad bedfellow, taking up half of the bed and snoring very loudly. But if I stay very very still under the covers, she will usually let me stay the night.

All in all, I am a happy and content little dog with a very big heart. I enjoy everything life brings my way, and Mom says that I am a very special house hound.

CHLOE

MACIE

I do not have any of those fancy registered titles that go with the many purebred dogs seen around Savannah. I am a rescue dog, and my mom, when asked, proudly says I am generic. Now I have no idea what "generic" means, but it must be a good thing because it always brings me a smile and many gentle pats on my head.

I do not know much about my past. I just know that the week before Christmas at the age of three months, my mom took me home to live with her. I am not certain of the exact date of my birth; my mom was told it was sometime in September. So to make remembering easy for mom, we claim 9/9/99 as my birthday. Each year on that date we celebrate with a homemade dog-food birthday cake and fresh-baked dog treats. The dogs in my neighborhood just love my birthday celebration because they all get "doggie bags" delivered to their front door.

My mom always takes me everywhere dogs are welcomed. I attend many of the outdoor cultural affairs sponsored by the city of Savannah. Each year I attend the Symphony in the Park and love to snuggle beneath the quilts under the stars. I do not attend the Mother's Day concerts in Morrell Park. The cannons that are fired during the 1812 Overture simply scare me to death. I often walk on the March of Dimes and Diabetes walks. Although dogs do not directly benefit from the cures, I figure that the more cures for people, the more rescues for us dogs. First Saturdays on River Street is always fun. The tourists get a big kick out of seeing me wear my hat as I stroll along the river-front. I suppose dogs in other cities do not wear hats, as the tourists are always asking to take my picture. I always agree to their requests. After all, life is pretty good for this ol' generic rescue dog.

MACIE

GINGER JOHNSON

I am a two-year-old Australian shepherd (Aussie). I live in Hinesville, Georgia, with a great family; we have been together since I was three months old. My family consists of my mom, dad, two sisters, and a very strange cat. My youngest sister, Jaime, picked me out because of my cute grin. My eldest sister loves for me to sit in her lap and get my tummy rubbed. My mom likes to see me do the infamous "Aussie wiggle butt," and my dad likes to see me do what they call the "crazy dog run." My buddy, Shady the cat, likes to fight with me. He seems to think he is beating me all the time, but I am really just letting him think that.

My mom says that I am your typical Aussie because I love to run and play. I spend most of my time in the house, stuck right next to my people, so they call me a Velcro dog. I follow them all around the house and sometimes end up in the bathroom with them, but I have learned to stay out of there. I love to play ball and Frisbee; my mom says that someday I will be a real Frisbee dog, whatever that means. My very favorite thing to do is to play in the water hose.

Before I came to live here, my mom was scared of dogs and claimed to be a cat person, but Dad and Jaime finally won her over to get a dog. When I came to live here, I was told I was going to be an outdoor dog, which was fine with me; but things have changed since then. Now I get to stay inside all day and sleep in the house, and sometimes I manage to sneak into the bed. I even get to help out less fortunate dogs because ever since she met me my mom has volunteered at the Humane Society and at Australian Shepherd Rescue. Every Saturday we take cans to the Humane Society, and my mom and sister walk the other dogs and play with them. Sometimes we take food and treats to them. We even have helped to transport a rescued Aussie to his foster family.

Last summer Shady was playing with a snake in the backyard. I went out to check out what was going on and ended up with a snakebite. Luckily I am a smart dog and was able to show my mom where that nasty snake bit me—on the nose. My family rushed me to the Emergency Veterinary Clinic. The bite hurt, I was scared, everyone was crying and driving fast; but it all turned out fine because the vet did a great job to get me well again. I learned a valuable lesson from that experience, and it also showed me how much my family loves me.

GINGER

ABBEY LEDESMA ("PRINCESS BUTTERCUP," "WHOVILLE GIRL," "DAIRY COW")

I consider myself a loving, playful golden retriever, who has several events that occur during the day that I am very passionate about. The first event is trying to arouse my mommy from her early morning sleep. Of course I always succeed at doing this by applying not one, not two, but three firm pats along her arm. If she tries to resist, I simply apply more pressure . . . oh, and a claw or two. Walla! Wide awake!

The next event is the daily bowl-licking relay, which takes place in one of the most wonderful places in the whole world—the kitchen. Always the source of food supply, the kitchen begins to have a certain aroma that is most familiar to me once my human has taken a bowl out of this black box that makes the food warm and mouth-watering to the senses. Once my mommy has finished her share of what she calls oatmeal, she always allows me to lap up what she is unable to finish. Yummy.

The last morning ritual, which I truly enjoy, is being let outside in my personal, fenced-in jungle—or as my humans call it, the backyard. This arena is my stomping ground, where I can chase squirrels, grab and devour sticks, swim in my poo,l and, very importantly, do my business. There was, however, one morning that will haunt me for the rest of my doggie years—one morning that will always leave me vulnerable to pure, unadulterated fear amongst the sound of any sudden, loud noise.

On that particular day I had successfully gotten through the early morning rituals with little to no trouble. As I proceeded to make my way outside into the jungle, I happened to notice that my mommy had placed a funny, shiny yellow covering over her body and another object that was round over her head. As she opened the door I leaped out with the usual innocent enthusiasm. Suddenly I realized that raindrops were wetting me. No problem. I actually liked playing in the rain because I'm always guaranteed a free towel massage once I come back in. I was anxiously roaming around the area, scoping out my territory, when suddenly *the incident* occurred. *Crackle! Boom!* Out of nowhere, this terrible, gut-wrenching explosion happened that seemed to be right over my head. I am a large girl, but can move and jump quickly when provoked. I think I cleared the ground by at least two feet, came back down, and made a beeline to the house. With my ears peeled back against my head, and eyes deliriously darting from side to side, I became as aerodynamic as a hundred-ten pound petite golden girl can. I sprinted full speed for the door, crashed into mommy's knees, and then proceeded to bank off every bit of furniture in the kitchen and hallway before I got to my final destination of sanctuary, my human's bed.

Even though I am older now and more mature, I still cringe when I hear loud noises from thunderstorms, when hunters around the area blast their guns, and when our neighbors ignite fireworks during holiday seasons. As scared as I get, I am comforted by the fact that my humans are always close by comforting and protecting me from harm's way.

ABBEY

Bambi Lazzaro ("Baby")

We have a new baby in our house. His name is Bambi because he looks just like a little deer.

You may remember, Pinocchio [see *Savannah Dogs*, pages 14–15], his famous older brother. I had been looking for another Italian greyhound to share Pinocchio's great life and to be his friend.

Bambi was a year old on March 28, 2001, and still is the very much spoiled, active baby. Pinocchio has not been happy with his new friend. Bambi will not let me out of his sight, so they both are under my feet all day. This has made Pinocchio very unhappy. He always had rested on his sofa all day, but nowadays he's on his feet when Bambi decides to rest. Poor, tired Pinocchio falls on the floor panting. I am grateful to be able to have my office in my home as both dogs are next to my chair all day.

For several years I wanted another dog like Pinocchio. My friend Julie, who is with Save-A-Life, called to tell me that my long wait was over. When Bambi came to live with us, he was well trained, smart, and beautiful. Now that he's settled in his new home and has taken over the whole place, he's very happy and everyone who comes to visit loves him. He's the joy of my life. Lately I haven't enjoyed going out because I miss my darling boys.

If you want lots of love and joy in your life, and have a place in your home and heart, please contact Save-A-Life. You just might fall in love.

SONYA LAZZARO

MATILLDA

This is the story of Matillda and how she came to be. I was a Marine on recruiting duty in Savannah. When I went to meet the family of a young man who had enlisted in the Marines, I was answered at the door by their English bulldog, Dog (pronounced "DeeOh-Gee"). After I concluded the welcoming of Ryan and his family to the Marine Corps, I commented on my desire to own a bulldog. Ryan's sister, Dana, told me they were going to visit the breeder from whom they got Dog. They would have invited me along, but on account of previous obligations could not. I told Dana to pick out a bulldog that she thought I would like and to save it for me. Billy, Dana's husband, asked if I thought I was ready to be a bulldog owner, not unlike the way I asked Ryan if he was ready to be a Marine.

Billy was also a former Marine and an alumnus of the University of Georgia. The English bulldog is the mascot of the United States Marine Corps. I didn't really have a name for the animal that would soon be running through my home, but had some ideas. Matilda is the name of a British tank of World War II. The name was both military and womanly in nature. I also

202

wanted it to be just a little uncommon. Dana and Billy got Matillda and her sister, Miss Georgia, and brought them to their house. When I first saw her, I knew I had named her properly because she looked like a Matilda tank. As Matillda grew, she started to go to work with me from time to time. Many people know her, if not by name, then by the sight of a Marine and a little bulldog. Soon she became part of the recruiting effort—not so much in the direct role, but in the building of rapport. This is an important thing to have as a recruiter. Matillda also had a knack for comforting a family. When young men and women are getting ready to go to boot camp at Parris Island, South Carolina, they bring their families to the office to see them off. When the families arrive at the office on Sunday mornings, it usually is an hour or more before the shuttle van arrives to go to Jacksonville, Florida. Matillda would be walking around the office on Montgomery Crossroads when the families arrived. She would seem to lighten the mood of a sad mother or girlfriend. The favorite thing for her was to chase empty twenty-ounce Coca-Cola bottles around the office.

I have since finished my tour as a recruiter, but still live in Savannah. I am currently assigned to the 2nd Beach and Terminal Operations Company, 4th FSSG, working with the Instructor-Inspector Staff, which trains Marine reservists at Hunter Army Airfield. Matillda accompanies me to work from time to time and spends the days chasing Chocolate, my cousin's dog, Dog, and Miss Georgia around their respective homes. Matillda is an outstanding companion, and I hope to enjoy her company for years to come.

GEOFFREY R. MARTZ

HENRY MACBETH

My wife and I were given a dog as a wedding present, believe it or not. Her name was Ginger, a beagle-dachshund mix. We both were working, and Ginger was losing attention to our first-born, so I thought she needed a friend. The Humane Society had an ad for "Henry" (a Manchester-dachshund mix) in the local *Pennysaver*, so I took Ginger to see if they would get along. Ginger ignored him, so I took him to the vet for a checkup before taking him home. The vet was so upset by the ticks and fleas that they gave me some dip and called the Humane Society to complain. In the car Henry quivered with fear and tried to hide, still not sure why. He's much better now, but still shakes at the sound of rain (impending thunder).

Due with our second child, my wife was amazed that I should bring home this scrawny, tick-scarred animal. She was especially impressed with the note from the Humane Society: "Nice dog, but becomes vicious around small children." Henry was wild; chewed everything, including concrete; tried to dig out numerous times; and peeled the vinyl off the cover of our hot tub. He has an impressive set of teeth and a quick reflex, but

204

he never has intentionally bit anyone. Like most dogs, however, he threatens anyone who approaches his food. It's best to drop a bit of food, as opposed to handing it to him.

Henry and Ginger initially enjoyed chasing each other in the yard or at the park. They were both built for speed—low to the ground and jacked-up in the rear. They also enjoyed their neighborhood walks and running free at the beach.

Sometimes I would forget to feed Henry, so he would help himself to a snake, dove, lizard, or whatever else he could find in the yard. Squirrels taunted Henry endlessly until one fell out of a tree. Henry ate the entire animal whole. I can still hear the bones crunching. Gross!

Ginger passed away last year at the ripe age of fourteen, so Henry was allowed to assume many of her indoor privileges. Most amazingly, although she once swore that Henry would be the last, my wife recently brought home Sally, a Chihuahua mix from Save-A-Life. You guessed it—"Henry met Sally." My wife decided that Henry needed a friend because he was still grieving over Ginger. Also, our youngest child has thoroughly enjoyed having a puppy around the house. Henry is about ten years old now, but seems to have regained his former playful self around Sally "the Rat." Henry barely recognizes Sally, now that she wears a lampshade from her recent encounter with an automobile.

Presently Henry is waiting for Sally to recover, and for some warm weather so they can frolic in the sun. Dogs are wonderful critters.

BEN MACBETH

205

FRITZ LEE SCHLAWINER ("FRITZ")

My life started on December 11, 2002, in Augusta, Georgia, the only son of Mom and Dad, miniature schnauzers. My new family in Savannah, Georgia, was so eager to get me home that I arrived five weeks later. My family thought long and hard about the perfect name for me. Because of my German ancestors, they chose Fritz. They should have chosen Boss because that's what I thought I was—the boss. I have a very stubborn and headstrong personality. Since I was an only son, it was my way or no way.

Little did my family or neighbors know what they were getting into when they invited me into their quiet lives. I definitely have tested their patience with my toilet-paper trick (tepeeing the house from the inside) and also with my uncontrollable barking and yelping. I just wish they knew that all I wanted was their un-divided attention. Well, I guess that I got their attention because I am now enrolled in military school, or obedience class. Whichever way you look at it, it's not much fun. It's been a long struggle, but we can see the light at the end of the tunnel.

One evening I overheard my family talking about getting me a playmate or partner in crime. I can hardly wait. I hope she likes me and looks like me. I have so many exciting things that I have learned and that I want to show her. For starters, how to get into the kitchen trash can and which sneakers taste the best, and my all-time favorite—the traumatization of our house cat, Sammy. I hope that my girlfriend likes my new home.

What a great place, Savannah—the new smells, the marsh at low tide, and the bright green rye grass in my own backyard. We already have started making additions to my yard. We are building a new wooden fence (white pickets) and new landscape just for me. It's so much fun helping out. I carry off the clippers and the pine straw; that's my job.

I live close to the river and already have made new friends: birds, raccoons, and squirrels. Last weekend we took our boat to Ossabaw Island on a fishing trip. It was a great experience, with the wind in my face and the cold saltwater spray. I hope that we go back soon and catch some fish.

Yesterday we went to downtown Savannah, where we stopped at Forsyth Park. I've never seen so many dogs at one time, all having so much fun playing Frisbee. I met a lot of Savannah natives, and they all had four paws.

Our last stop was River Street, where everything was green in preparation for the big day, St. Paddy's Day. I'm afraid that I'm too young to mingle, but I hope that we will go to the parade. I've never been dyed green.

During my short three months, I've seen and done a lot. Savannah is a great place to grow up, and I'm looking forward to a long and happy life with my new family. Hope to see y'all soon.

FRITZ

207

ALEX SHEFFIELD

At the age of thirteen I moved to Savannah to live with my "grandparents" on Skidaway Island. The lifestyle here is definitely slow and easy. Many humans ride in golf carts while their dogs walk beside the cart on a leash. It's been quite an adjustment for me since my "parents," Karen and Randy, moved to Scotland. I understand from all the talk by my human "mom" and "dad" that I could have gone, but I would have been in a cage for six months. I overheard them say that they just didn't have the heart to put me through British quarantine. It's been said that I'm deaf; I can, however, still hear thunder and the snapping of fingers. I think I just have "selective hearing." I also have weakness in my back legs and have walking problems. I can't walk very far, and I have to have help getting up the smallest step; but if you say the word "go," I'm at the front door in no time at all.

My life began in North Georgia, near Athens. My mom was in veterinary school at the University of Georgia at the time, so as a six-week-old puppy I became her first patient. She used me to practice her doctoring skills. Initially I was quite a handful. My mom even thought of giving me away the first year since I just wouldn't listen to her. She was glad she kept me because I became her best friend. I helped her get through veterinary school, which she says is quite hard. Later I became a blood donor for other dogs who were sick or injured. I have nice big veins, and I was an "easy stick," I heard her say.

Soon after graduation we moved to Charleston, South Carolina, where we had fun swimming in the ocean together. My mom was never afraid to go out at night to treat sick horses because she had me to protect her. We enjoyed walks on The Battery at night. I tried to jump out of the back of a moving pickup truck one day. After that my mom would cross-tie me so I could not jump out.

After Charleston my human parents married and we three moved to Houston, Texas. It was much hotter in Texas, but I had a big fenced-in backyard to play in. My favorite thing to do was to chase squirrels. I did a good job of keeping them out of my yard. There was a pond behind the house with a dock, and occasionally I got to go out and see the alligators. There was also a raccoon that came though the yard every day. I loved riding in the car, so the long rides out to the ranch to see our horse, James, were the best part of my day. After my human sibling Erin was born, we made lots of trips to the barn. I was a great protector. I didn't really mind it at all when Erin crawled all over me or used me to hold on to when she was learning to walk.

It took three days of traveling to come to Savannah. Of course I didn't know that my mom would be leaving me with my grandparents. I was quite sad for the first week, but soon began to enjoy being the spoiled, only grand-dog. My favorite toy is a freshly opened can of tennis balls. My favorite activity is to lie in front of the foyer windows and watch the squirrels in the front yard. At night my grand-mom takes me in her car to the marina to see the other dogs; and because she has to lift me into the car, this is not always easy. Did I mention that I weigh a hundred pounds? My grandparents have taken me into their home and their hearts. I wish I could say the same for Morris, their thirteen-year-old, orange, tabby cat. Morris has to stay outside, because on the very first day that I arrived he attacked me. This could have been disastrous, but I have such a thick, shiny, black coat, that Morris could not get a hold of my skin.

I've lived a long life so far. If I were human, I'd be at least ninety-one. Most people are amazed when told how old I am. They say I'm in such good shape and that German shepherds don't usually live to be that old. I don't really feel old, but I guess that my white whiskers give me away.

ALEX

HUGO MACDONALD

My name is Hugo, and this is the story of how I came to live in Savannah with a new owner. A year and a half ago I was adopted, rescued. That is when my new life began. I am now three years old, and my previous owner was a military man stationed in Europe. Since I am a Scottish terrier, my heritage is Celtic from the Highlands of Scotland. My actual lineage is Eastern European. I was born in Hungary and lived with my previous owner in Italy.

During the fall of 2000, we moved to Savannah. It was a very tiring trip—two plane flights from Italy to Savannah. I traveled in the baggage compartment because I weighed two pounds too much to be in the passenger cabin. It was lonely. We arrived safely, and by Christmastime my military man received his new assignment and pets were not allowed. It was a sad day. I needed a new home or I would be sent to an animal shelter or to some other unmentionable fate. Through some friends we were introduced to Alice, a lady who had owned a girl Scottie for fifteen years and was anxious to have another. It was difficult and sad that my first owner had to give me away, but I was given to

211

someone who really wanted me and takes great care of me.

When I first arrived at Alice's home, I know she thought about changing my name to something more Scottish sounding, like Duncan or Cameron or Campbell. It just never happened. I am glad I got to keep my name, Hugo, because it suits me. Soon I met some of the neighbors. They thought that I was quite handsome and very friendly. They were all very nice to me. Since moving to the Historic District, my life has been wonderful. I have a courtyard to play in, safe from traffic, and there are nice parks to visit. In the squares we meet other dogs. There are many dogs in my neighborhood, and some are really friendly and playful. There are also squirrels to chase, birds to watch, flowers to sniff, and the occasional cat to bark at. I love our walks, except in the rain. I hate getting my feet wet. The walks that are the most fun of all are the visits to the many shops where they give dog treats. Savannah is a very dog-friendly city. The only thing I cannot do is go to restaurants and cafés, like I did in Italy.

I love living in my new city and home. Life could not be better. I sleep on my owner's bed, have lots of play toys, and am allowed to sit on the furniture. During most evenings we sit together and read or watch TV. Sometimes we watch movies. I like *Shrek* the best, especially the little donkey. I am glad I live here and so is my new owner.

HUGO

HERSCHEL

At long last this book provides the chance of a lifetime to get a few things off my chest. For example, it really frosts my double-curled tail when my owner tells someone, "If there *is* such a thing as reincarnation, I'd like to come back as a pug." He blithely overlooks all the things I have to do *every single day*: (1) scare horses off Washington Square by barking up a storm as they approach; (2) water every tree in Emmett Park; (3) keep squirrels from trespassing and trampling the grass; (4) greet house visitors with a shoe in my mouth; (5) guard the entrance after my owners leave, vigilantly positioned on the hall rug until I hear the key in the lock; (6) deposit hair on every square inch of the floor so they can tell what's been vacuumed as they clean house; (7) consume every chicken part, French fry, among other food that careless diners leave around the sidewalk; and (8) set a good "responsible pug" example for my little sister in every possible way. There's more, but suffice it to say it's a real struggle to pack it all into a day and still sneak in my nineteen hours of beauty sleep.

This past year was especially tough because of the

213

eyelid surgery (with no time off). That plastic cone thing placed around my neck to protect the stitches was a total fiasco. Pugs basically have no noses, yet I love to sniff. No, actually I live to sniff. That first night after the operation I hustled up to the telephone pole to see who had been around—and crashed the cone right into it. Yikes! To this day I'm not sure the vertebrae have settled back into place. That had to be one of the most jarring events of my life, perhaps matched only by falling through the pond ice in Wisconsin when I went after some ducks and geese that were teasing me. Oh, speaking of "jarring" experiences, the all-time high in that category must be the arrival of Mini-me.

Mini-me [see pages 216–18] would be my little sister. She has *way* too much energy, and always needs to get her way and have the last word. I love her dearly, and we are inseparable; but aren't there some "pug chill pills" they could give her to prevent that annoying whirling dervish thing she does? Sure, it's great that she loves life and just can't get enough excitement (or enough of anything else). But *when* is she going to get a grip? It's not like me to snort my own praises, but I am the picture of poise and composure compared to Mini-me.

How to explain my mature outlook and steady temperament? Well, I am seven already, and I've been around. Born in Montana, I took a plane ride to my Illinois house in the woods as a baby (or, I guess that would be "puppy," even though Carol says Mini and I are "her babies"). Ah, those woods, with trees every-where to be watered. I had to become very systematic and learn to "conserve" as I sprinkled, so I could mark as many as possible. Then I moved to a townhouse in

214

downtown Milwaukee, where I trained on barking (majoring in Harleys and those fireworks they have every weekend all summer). And now Savannah. I guess Dad must be what people call "retired," because now *he* gets to walk me all the time. Retirement is an alien concept in pugdom; something I can only dream about. But I can't even dream for long because here comes another horse carriage with a load of tourists on board. Excuse me. I need to get back to work, and then I'll need a treat.

For your convenience, please refer to my list of most valuable treats: (1) dried lamb lungs (Pam, the nice neighbor lady, has some); (2) pigs' ears (I get one whenever Mom and Dad have dinner); (3) cheese (well, after all, I did live in Wisconsin); (4) raw cabbage (do not mix in the lettuce, because I know the difference); (5) broccoli stalks (good for my heart, you know); and (6) whatever is left on your plate (conserve water and electricity by replacing your dishwasher with a pug).

HERSCHEL

215

MINI-ME

My brother, Herschel [see pages 213–15], has it made living here in Georgia, where his namesake, Herschel Walker, is a legend. Me? I am cursed by my name, which is Mini-me. Mom and Dad thought that I would look like the "Hersch man" (as I like to call him), only smaller. So I just have to keep showing that I'm really a very big dog—in spirit, in energy, in fearlessness (vocally), and in the way I can totally disrupt the lives of all around me. Does the word "overcompensating" mean anything to you?

I chuckle-snort when they tell people, "She still has a lot of puppy in her." Guess again, you silly humans. This *is* me, I'm two already, and if you think I am *ever* going to slow down (even in the heat and humidity of Savannah), you simply don't know the meaning of the term "joy of life." I figure that they can always throw me in the tub to cool me down because my job basically is to rev things up. I'm running when you are walking. You stroll past the stoops on houses, but I bound up and down them. You sit; I bounce. You relax and I lick you. I crane my neck to look around while you rest your head on a pillow. In Pooh terms, I am a combination of Tigger and Roo. My low gear is higher than your overdrive. "Mini-me," indeed! How about something like "Max Force" or "Maxed Out"? That's the *real* me. I wish that Savannah had some snow drifts like I used to dive into in Wisconsin—don't you?

Everyone was put on earth for a reason. Mine was clear from the day I came to live with Herschel (now seven years of age), who was way too serious and overburdened by responsibilities he had taken on. I began his therapy by jumping over him, crawling under him, wrestling with him while chomping on his collar, licking his face, and crashing into him when he tries to sniff or pee. One day he was sniffing in the yard when I wanted to play. He didn't pay any attention to my antics and yipping until I jumped him from behind and pushed him right into the flower bed with my front feet. That got his attention, although the outcome was not terribly pleasant for me. He nailed me pretty good with that big solid head of his, right into the fence. Still, whenever Herschel is trying to snuggle up to Carol on the couch, I kamikaze my way between them. That's a blast.

Herschel had this really polite way of patiently waiting for a treat after a walk. That's baloney; they might forget, you know. So I showed him how you could sprint across the kitchen and fling yourself against the cabinet door, where treats are "hidden" (as if we could not figure that out, for crying out loud). And after dinner he would just look hopeful when they started cleaning off the plates. Forget that. I showed Hersch how to dance around on his hind legs, all shrieking and squealing, until the table scraps are delivered hastily to their rightful owners—us.

217

I'm told that big brother Herschel was even afraid to go out on the second-floor balcony until I came. Well, now they have protective wire all around the lower part of the ironwork because I had this idea it might be very cool to hurl myself down into one of those horse carriages going by. Now Herschel will go out on the balcony in a heartbeat to look around or sun himself, but he never would have learned without me to show him the way.

So keep your eye out for me. I'm not going to be overlooked just because I got shortchanged in the size department. As long as they are putting pugs in movies like *Men in Black*, *Milo and Otis*, and *Best in Show*, I just know there's a place for me—as a Hollywood stunt pug—among the rich and famous. Herschel may get the serious acting parts because he can be so dignified looking; but when it comes to action flicks, I'm the one you want. Let's see—"Crouching Poodle, Leaping Pug." Has a nice ring to it, no? Now . . . let's get crazy!

For the record, I do endorse Herschel's entire "list of most valuable treats." Which reminds me, I'm hungry. Got anything to share with a growing (I wish) young chick?

MINI-ME

HOPE WOLF

In August 2000 I lived in a drainage ditch with my five puppies. It wasn't much, but it was shelter. My human seemed to care less, so I decided to go it alone. Me and my five beautiful baby boys. Living on leaves, grass, and twigs was tough. I felt thin and weak, but my little ones had to nurse and survive.

One day a compassionate human found us. Hopeful but cautious, we went to a place called the Humane Society. What a great place—food, attention, dry warm bed. Sure beat the old drainage ditch.

They said that I had something bad called "heartworms" and that I might never see my babies grow. Not one to give up hope, I looked at the humans with as much courage and determination as I could muster.

They said I had something called "fortitude." Must be a good thing because they said there was hope for me. A kindhearted human, Mary Peabody, vowed that she'd make sure heartworms wouldn't be the end of me. But first, Mary said, I'd go to a "foster home" until my babies were weaned. Another lady-human came to look at us. As she heard our story, her eyes became very soft.

Her name was Terry Wolf, and she said that we were going home with her.

Foster homes are great. Immediately I felt safe when I saw the happy faces of other dogs there. Terry gave us a secluded room, fresh water, and food, and stroked my face and belly until I'd fall asleep. She said I must have had lots of "resolve." She called me "Hope" because she said that's what helped me survive.

Soon people came to see how beautiful my boys had become. They were even on television. Stars. "Perfect Pets" they were called. They each left with nice, loving families. I'd miss them, but I was now too tired for their energy. Terry said I'd done a wonderful job with my boys, but now I needed my "fortitude" to help myself.

It took courage, but I had the best doctor. Dr. Karen Kane helped rid my body of the horrible heartworms. What a gentle, loving hand she has. Even today I secretly enjoy going to see her.

Soon I felt like my old self. There was no more coughing, and my coat was brilliant and I'd gained weight. I played with Terry's other dogs and began to feel like I was part of her pack.

One day Mary said a family might want to adopt me. As Mary took me away to meet them, Terry watched. Her soft eyes were now wet. Now *she* needed "Hope."

Don't get me wrong. The people were very nice. Delicate glass things around their quiet, neat home. Hmmm . . . Well, I started acting happy, jumpin' around, showing them all my energy. Must've been a bit too much for them. I couldn't wait until we got back home. Home. My home. I knew it when I saw

Terry—still waiting outside, hoping I would come home.

Today I have my own special spot in the corner, my own bowls, my very sacred leash, and I've never been happier. I'm the top protector of Terry's pack, which is an odd mixture of humans and other rescued dogs, and we're all very content. Now, when a new "foster" arrives, I'm there first—sharing kibble, playing chase. It's my turn to reassure them that their days of fear and desperation are behind them, and that if you nuzzle that soft-eyed lady, she'll spoil you like the royalty you are.

HOPE

MOLLY WHITE

On paper my name reads "Lil Booger Bear." I am often referred to as "Lovey," "Angel," and "Tootie Bell." So you see, it is no wonder that I don't listen sometimes, with all those names. Don't get me wrong, I am a very good dog, not your everyday dog; and I am very beautiful, if I must say so. A black-and-tan Pomeranian, I am—black shiny coat with a tan scarf. Can you imagine being born with such natural beauty?

I was born into this world on June 3, 1997, in a litter of only two. So you see, I am almost one of a kind. At six weeks of age I was adopted by two of the most wonderful parents any girl could ask for—John and Kathy White of Savannah. I am nearly human, and if you stick around awhile, I will begin to explain.

I lead a rather elegant lifestyle, if I must say so. My mom and dad work, so I have the house all to myself most of the day. Every now and then, Dad pops in to say hello and then be on his way. In my house there are lots of windows where I always know what is going on outside, but have the pleasure of never getting overheated or too cool. Occasionally I will take a short nap on the couch in the living room, but I always have an ideal view of the front door.

It is not until much later in the day that my mom arrives home. When she comes in the door, I am so glad to see her; she makes me start howling. My mom tells me that she can be in a bad mood from work, come home, see me, and everything is all better.

At night I get to sleep with my parents in their bed. I am so lucky to have my own pillow and blanket. This is probably the most favorite time of the day for me. I get to spend the whole night with both of my parents, and in the morning I can shower them with my many sweet kisses.

I love to play, and I have a toy box full of all kinds of squeaky animals. My mom brings me home a new toy at least once a month, so I never get bored.

There is a huge fenced-in backyard where I can run, play, and feel very safe. A ton of squirrels come and visit me every day. I love to chase after them, and they like it too.

Even though I might be on what you call a special diet, I get hand-fed twice a day. Sometimes my mom might give me a piece of toast. (I love toast, and my very favorite is banana Popsicles.)

Sometimes I take an occasional stroll down Savannah's own River Street, and oh, how I enjoy that. You would too if everywhere you went people stopped to ooh and ah over you.

I am groomed at Dr. Case's office about every six weeks. How I hate that. But, nevertheless, it is only for a day; and when it is all said and done, I am once again most beautiful. My dad picks me up at the end of the day, and, boy, am I glad to see him, because I know I am going to . . . home sweet home.

I will soon turn five years old. Boy, how time flies when you're having fun. Certainly I have loved every minute of my life. How could one be so lucky to have a loving home and such a great life. Wouldn't you agree?

Very fortunately,

MOLLY

GILHAVEN'S SUPERNATURAL D-LITE ("HARRY POTTER")

What's going on? My whole world is changing. I'm being pushed down a chute. I don't really want to leave this wonderful world, where everything is quiet, subdued, and serene. Hey, cut that out. Quit pushing. Wait, what's this? A new sensation. Soft and warm, loving, and yet very invigorating. Hmmm, a comfy back massage. Now a gentle tummy rub. I love these new feelings. I sense they're coming from a source that loves me, too. Maybe I should just go ahead and draw my first breath, and check out what's going on in this new world that I have just been so unceremoniously dumped into.

Hello? Mama? Is that you? I'm hungry. Where are those bottles? I gotta go potty. Where are some other warm bodies to cuddle up to? What? I'm your only one? How special does that make me!

My birthday was a very special day, not only for my mama Becca and me, but for my dad too. My birthday was Saturday, November 17, 2001. Yep, that's right. The very day of the book signing for *Savannah Dogs* at Barnes & Noble. My dad, Sandpiper's Furst Romance, has a story in the first *Savannah Dogs* [see pages

234–37]. My human mama's son, Jimmy, had to take my dad to the book signing so she could stay home and wait for me to be born.

My mama loves me. She spends most of my waking moments with me. During the day, when she leaves my whelping box for a minute, I squirm way over to one side to sleep under the pig rail up against the wall. In my puppy dreams I am snuggled up with my sisters and brothers. When my human mama comes home after work, at first she can't find me. When she finally does, she has to squeeze me out from under the rail, and that is getting tough to do because I am getting so big now. At night, after I fall asleep, my mama slips out of my whelping box and hops up on the bed for some real relaxation and attention from our human mama. But as soon as I wake up, all hungry and crampy, I just let out a tiny little cry and like a flash my mama is off that bed and right next to me in the box, cleaning me, feeding me, keeping me warm, loving me. I have the most wonderful mama in the whole world.

Check this out. At ten days old, I was the first puppy in my litter to open my eyes, the first one to let loose with that adorable little three-week-old puppy bark, the first one to climb out of the litter box before I even knew where I was going or why I wanted to go there. I just knew that I wanted to sleep on the outside of the box. I am the smartest, the prettiest, and the best, and my mama loves me the most in the whole litter.

Wait, what's this? There's one right between my eyes. Another in the crook of my baby neck. Kisses? My human mama sure shows affection in strange ways. I can't help but wonder why she doesn't just pee-pee on the bed or chew up a shoe.

226

Haaaaarrrrry! What? Who's that? *Me*? But I'm playing with the cat, running big circles in the yard with my mama, chewing up sticks. So much to do, I just don't have time to come.

Uh-oh, I've turned around and my human mama's gone. Where did she go? I must barrel my chubby self down the hall to see if she's trying to put on her socks without me swinging from the toes. Not there, Maybe she's trying to slip into those jeans without me playing tug of war with one of the legs. Maybe I lost her in the bathroom; I need to finish "reading" that dog magazine, too. What if she drops her shoes on the floor and I'm not there to run off with one of them? Don't you know how important timing is? Not every puppy can handle all this tough stuff. Oh, there she is on the couch. And now here I am, too, curling up beside her and putting my little head on a pillow so I can just lie there and gaze up at her. Do you wonder how I got so spoiled?

My human mama was worried that because I was the only puppy in my litter I might grow up to be a big yellow freakazoid, so she took me to day-care at the Canine Education Center when I was just eleven weeks old. I know she worried all day that someone might pick on me or that I might hide in a corner and chew my nails. Not so. When she came to pick me up, there I was, right smack in the middle of thirty-six of the best friends I've ever had.

So many glorious and wonderful things have happened to me in my first twelve weeks of life. The world is truly my oyster, and I am truly the pearl in my mama's life.

HARRY POTTER

CEDAR LYNN
SWEENEY-REEVES
("C.C.")

Once upon a time, the mamas had a pond. It was *my* pond, and my older brother and sisters respected that. They didn't like to swim anyway, so they'd just wade up to their chest and leave the serious swimming and diving to me. I was the master diver, too. I'd wait until Mama Mary got really wound up. (I think that she actually believed she was winding *me* up.) Then, when she would finally throw the ball, I would launch from the highest bank I could find and make a tremendous splash. The mamas would oooh and aaaah and tell me how good I was. They were pretty well trained to keep throwing the ball until all of us were muddy and soaked to the bone. I think that I smelled great that way, but they always wanted to give the dreaded bath (the only four-letter word that really bothers me.) Still the game was pretty fun.

Then, one day, the mamas brought not one, but two, obnoxious ankle biters and introduced them as the new babies. The mamas explained that they thought I needed younger siblings to play with. I tried to explain to the mamas that they were my playmates and that I was fine with that. Anyway, these two furballs were

228

introduced as Rowdy and Ursa. I knew they were trouble the minute they tried to follow me into the pond. This was my pond and they were interlopers.

They were actually pretty good swimmers, being part Labrador retriever. I would not admit that to anyone, but other dog lovers and I never told the mamas I actually liked them. They were, in fact, the reason I learned my most amazing trick.

We were all at the pond one day, and the brats were swimming farther and farther out each time the ball was thrown. I even thought they might beat me to it one day, and that made me worried. The mamas thought it would be cute to see if the newcomers would actually go all the way to the ball and bring it back, so they put *me*, the only true ball chaser, on a down-stay on the bank. They threw the ball for the other dogs. I couldn't believe it. I knew there must be some mistake, so as the puppies were struggling toward the ball I snuck and launched my highest dive ever. Mama Charra busted me out of the corner of her eye and yelled, "Cedar, no!" When I hit the water, I was facing the shore and dog paddling for all I was worth. I had performed the first in-flight reverse one-eighty with a twist.

I thought I was in big trouble, but the mamas were so busy laughing at my amazing "trick" that I never even got a lecture. I decided right then, there might be benefits to having younger siblings. The mamas are *still* impressed with my quick response and still get jollies out of watching me launch. They've never made me do the trick again, but I could if I wanted to.

CEDAR

DARIEN SOKOLOWSKI
("DARI")

Darien came into my life unexpectedly nine years ago. On my way to St. Simons Island to visit a friend, I decided to stop just outside the town of Darien for a rest break. While standing by the water's edge, this small emaciated dog came up to me. She was nothing but skin and bones. It was obvious to me that she had just given birth to a litter and had not eaten in a long time. She was whimpering and somewhat afraid. I felt so bad seeing this dog in such a miserable condition that I decided to put her in the car and take her to the Humane Society in Brunswick to have her put to sleep. Before leaving the marsh I spent some time looking for her puppies, but to no avail.

When I arrived in Brunswick the Humane Society was closed. So I bought a can of dog food, and the rest is history. *From a swamp dog to a princess.* Darien spent the night in a cardboard box at the foot of my bed. The next morning we returned to the marsh where I had found Darien, thinking that she would go to her puppies if there were any. She would not leave my side, so we continued on to Savannah. Our first stop was the vet's. After she had a thorough exam and spent the night for observation, and after a considerable bill, I had myself a new pet. My decision to keep Darien has never been regrettable.

Darien is a small beagle–Jack Russell type. She is affectionate and very spoiled. Darien loves to be petted and rubbed, and enjoys snuggling up to me, but to this day does not like to be picked up. When she is picked up, she becomes rigid and stiff. Darien has learned how to wrap me around her paws, so much so that I almost have to get her permission to get into my own bed. Darien refuses to sleep at the foot of the bed these days, preferring to be enthroned on the pillows at the head.

ROBERT F. SOKOLOWSKI

LA's Gracie Mae ("Boogie Bear")

My given name is LA's Gracie Mae, but I have come to be known as Boogie Bear. Don't ask me how that happened. Sometimes humans are so strange, but I wouldn't trade my girl for the world. I'll never forget the day I was chosen for the Smith pack. My owner-to-be came into the pet store simply to browse and unwind after work. I looked on in dismay as the girl asked the clerk to bring out my next-door neighbor, for she had caught the girl's eye. That mutt was always a showboat, if you ask me. I watched them disappear into the play area. I was heartbroken. Perhaps it was the fact that I was a cocker spaniel with an underbite that would rival the whole UGA family put together. I think the fact that I can't put my bottom teeth in my mouth is all part of my endearing charm. As I sat there, I began to question my AKC lineage. I mean, it is a possibility that one of those bulldogs trespassed one evening on the "puppy farm." Who knows? Hey, maybe I could get some season tickets out of that.

Suddenly the girl of my dreams emerged from the play pen with a look of utter disgust on her face and handed that meddling mongrel back to the store clerk.

That was my big chance to prove that my need for dental care had no bearing on the fact that I was the dog for her. I began to scratch the glass with a vengeance. I nearly fainted. The girl just turned and walked away. I could not believe it. My irritating neighbor stuck her tongue out at me. Some pooches are so uncouth. I gave one last hopeful glance over my shoulder, and low and behold, the girl did the same. I panicked. I had a split second to win her heart, and I was at a loss for what to do. I was blowing it. I did the first thing that entered my mind. In complete desperation, I licked the glass. Would you believe it actually worked? Next thing I knew, I was being rung up at the register. To my knowledge, there was no extra charge for the underbite.

My new owner took me to our new home. It was the biggest kennel I had ever seen. My little nose nearly fell off as I attempted to sniff over every nook and cranny. Don't ask me why; that's just what dogs do. Finally I had succumbed to the excitement of what I later referred to as "liberation day." I collapsed from exhaustion. As if the sheer jubilation of the freedom was not enough, my girl went out and hunted for me while I was asleep. Can you believe the loyalty? She hunted food that came neatly in cans (which is a lot less messy than the old days), a bag of treats, a shiny new tennis ball, and the most amazing squeaky toy ever invented, Mr. Lion.

I am almost three years old now, and I have a toy box full of squeaky toys, but none has held a candle to my Mr. Lion. Maybe I love him so because he reminds me of that glorious day or just because he reminds me of how much my girl loves me, underbite and all. All I know is that Mr. Lion and my girl make me wag my little tail so fast and with such fury that I fear it may come loose from my behind. That has to be a good sign.

BOOGIE BEAR

SIMONE
MUHLENKAMP

Simone Muhlenkamp is an exquisite basset hound and a true Southern lady. A one-time Atlanta resident, Simone is now the darling of Savannah.

After Simone's former owner passed away last year, she found herself stranded at the dog pound. It soon became clear that the pound was no place for this five-year-old basset beauty with the world's most gentle disposition. Basset Hound Rescue of Georgia whisked Simone off to safety and placed her in a loving foster home until she could be adopted. I saw the picture that Simone's foster mom had posted on the BHRG website and immediately fell in love. I convinced my husband, David, that a basset hound would be the perfect addition to our family, and in no time we were off to Atlanta to adopt Simone.

When David and I brought Simone to our townhouse on Gaston Street, we were excited, but cautious at the same time. She was recovering from heartworm treatment and was physically weak as a result. Confused by her new surroundings, Simone spent much of her time either sleeping or just lying around. We never lost faith, however, that Simone would brighten up. On the second day she rolled over on her back for us to pet her. One week later she joyfully greeted me at the door when I returned home from work. As Simone sprinted around me in circles, I knew that she had found her forever-family.

Her personality has truly blossomed since then. Still an extraordinarily tranquil dog, Simone has also revealed her penchant for treats, chew bones, leash walks, chasing squirrels in Forsyth Park, and, most of all, attention. Luckily for Simone, her long ears and soulful eyes attract plenty of attention. When Simone senses that humans are whispering about her, she will immediately prance over to her admirers and sit down to be petted. She also loves accompanying us to downtown restaurants that have outdoor seating. I have to laugh when tour buses pass by and the passengers seem more interested in Simone than in Savannah's historic landmarks.

Of course some of Simone's most memorable moments in Savannah have occurred during the city's special festivities. On St. Patrick's Day she wore a shamrock bandanna and watched the parade from the sidelines. We brought her downtown that evening, and she quickly became a crowd favorite. She even ended up being featured on one tourist's home video. After her St. Patrick's Day debut, Simone made an appearance at the Savannah College of Art and Design's Sidewalk Arts Festival. She had so much fun playing with the other dogs at the festival and meeting people from around the world. That evening, after the festival was over, Simone and I went back to the park and marveled at the beautiful student artwork.

Simone is very content with her life in Savannah,

and she in turn brings joy to many people each day. David and I will always be grateful to Basset Hound Rescue for giving Simone a second chance.

KATHERINE E. MUHLENKAMP

BEAR OF MONTEREY SQUARE

I am Bear of Monterey Square,
Mr. Bear,
Pooh Bear, Pretty Bear,
Honey Bear, Happy Bear,
Bear Nuckle, Snuckle Bear,
Sweet Bear, Care Bear,
Old Bear, New Bear,
Funny Bear, Chickie Bear,
Polar Bear, Teddy Bear,
Fuzzy Bear, Wuzzy Bear,
Bear Naked, Baby Bear,
Dancing Bear, Wonder Bear,
All of these and more!

In my youth, I, Bear that I am—named for my resemblance to a bear cub—would escape my pen with my playmate, Vincent, a Siberian husky. We would get into mischief aplenty. I was known to have a certain affinity for long streaming pajama bottoms, slips, long johns, and the like, hanging on neighbors' clotheslines. I would wrestle them to the ground and tear through the neighborhood, waving my prize behind me like a flag of victory. What trouble would ensue as the garment would be in shreds when I finished my parade. Vincent and I had many such jolly times together until one day we both ran off in opposite directions. He seemed to vanish into thin air. I was so engrossed in my meandering that I didn't seem to notice immediately that he was gone. Nor did I realize that I had wandered so far from home. I didn't recognize where I was. 'Twas no matter, I was more interested in a good time and a good meal. I knew that people would be my source for both, and so I looked for the nearest person to attach myself to when hunger and thirst overtook my innate desire for fun. Sure enough, I found two such good kind souls who put out a tasty meal and water; but for reasons that were unclear to me, they didn't open their home completely. These folks already had an older dog and weren't ready for a new member, so I was left to fend for myself. I found a friendly, cozy corner close by and curled up for the night.

In the morning, when I awoke, I was feeling a little lonely, a bit chilly, bewildered, and weepy. I tried to keep up a good front and went in search of my destiny. Eventually I found a young couple playing Frisbee, and with all the charm I could muster, I joined in. They seemed to like me well enough, but when it was time for them to depart, the truth came out. It seems a little girl was anxious, beyond words, to pet me. Her mother, being cautious, was hesitant to let her do so until she gained permission from the young couple with whom I was playing. Upon further investigation, the young couple divulged my greatest secret—I didn't belong to them. At this point they very gallantly left me and the Frisbee in the care of the little girl and her mother.

By and by the little girl and her mother took me home, but again, I was not allowed entrance into the house. This time it was out of concern for my original owners. These folks thought that if I could be spotted by passersby, then my former owners, who could very well be out searching, would have a better chance of finding me. All day I remained in the front garden finding shady spots in which to keep cool, faithfully waiting, wondering and watching each and every activity that was happening in and out of the house.

It was a long day—probably the longest I had ever known. As night fell and the lights went on inside the house, I continued to watch. Then it dawned on the occupants inside that no one could see me in the dark outside. Since I was so faithful as to be out there all this time, never stirring from my post, it was time to take me in for the night. Thanks, God.

As it turns out, this little girl was the youngest of six children and I was in puppy heaven with all these youngers to play with! Yes, they did take me in, forever. I was a proud and happy puppy to have such a large family of which to be a part. My former owners were, indeed, found and gave me over with loving approval as they knew how much I adored children. Vincent too was found and was safely back in their keeping. They decided that one dog was enough.

My family, however, doesn't believe in such bunk, and has since welcomed two lovely ladies: one black, Sasha, and one tan, Daphne [see *Savannah Dogs*, pages

211–15], to keep me company. I rule the roost at, now, fourteen years old. We trot around Forsyth Park twice daily as a threesome, and I do believe that I am still young for all of it.

BEAR

·

FRIENDLY
SUSSMAN

Hi! Through my dog network, I heard about this little girl who always wanted a puppy named Friendly. I knew that I had to have that name. I knew that I could live up to it. I used the same dog network (*very* top secret) to get the message to her, and it worked. I became that little girl's present on her fifth birthday. I was so lucky.

The family came all the way to South Carolina to get me. I was a little shy and scared at first, but I knew I could do it. I rode in the car for five long hours to get to my new home in Savannah. I was so excited. My new home was great. There was a big backyard with bushes to hide in, grass to dig up, and flowers to eat. It was heaven.

Once I was settled in my new home, I became less shy. I started to enjoy my family. No one could have better friends than Sophie and her sister, Claire. They both love to hug me and play with me. One day we even had a tea party on the kitchen floor. I had a really hard time getting my nose in that little teacup, though. We play chase, fetch, and so many other games. I am not allowed to play with Barbies anymore. Sophie's mom did not think that chewing the Barbies was a part of the game. The best game of all is called Stealing. My favorite things to steal are stuffed animals and Claire's blanket. I sneak up, steal, and then the chase is on.

When I am not playing, I like to sleep. In fact the vet said that I was the laziest beagle he had ever seen. I'm not quite sure if that was a compliment.

I had a great life. I really had it made. My family loved me and I was the center of attention. They took me for walks, played with me, scratched my belly, and did everything else a puppy could want. Then one day it all changed. Claire turned five and got a little gray tabby kitten for her birthday. She named the kitten Princess. My family loved her too, and I was not sure that I liked that. I took all of her toys, chased her under a chair, and would not let her out. But soon I realized that I really liked the cat. We became best friends. We share meals, play chase, and sleep together. Princess also likes to give me a bath every day. Life would be boring without her.

All in all, I have had a great two years with my family. I just knew that I could be a dog called Friendly. I am friendly with everyone—cats, dogs, and people. But I have a special place in my heart for children. The name Friendly fits me and I am proud of it. Thanks, Sophie.

FRIENDLY

BEARFOOT

We first got Bearfoot the day we found out we were pregnant with our first child. He was to be a crash course in responsibility for two young twenty-somethings celebrating their first wedding anniversary and a surprise pregnancy. We had gone to Warm Springs, Georgia, to visit Johnny Wilkes at the Good Shepherd Riding Academy, a magical farm where handicapped children ride horses just a stone's throw from FDR's Little White House. In cases where the child can't sit, he is laid like a sack of potatoes over the horse's back, then the horse carries his precious cargo ever so gingerly around the barnyard. Many of the animals on Johnny's farm had handicaps, such as the one-legged duck and the turkey that had been fed so many steroids that he was more top-heavy than Dolly Parton. Special children could identify with these special animals.

Johnny had found Bearfoot and his brother abandoned on the side of the road in rural Merriweather County. Bearfoot was about six weeks old and the cutest little yellow dog with the biggest paws you ever saw. We suspected he was a Lab-retriever mix, but we knew he was destined to be a good yellow dog. Bear-

244

foot instinctively knew we were his people. On his tiny, puppy legs, he followed us like a soldier as we rode our horses across Pine Mountain.

That night in the Presidential Suite at the Roosevelt Inn in downtown Warm Springs, we could talk of nothing but that dog. Perhaps it was because he closely resembled my husband's childhood dog, Barley, whom his parents "sent away to live on a nice farm" after he bit the mailman. Perhaps we were simply terrified at the prospects of caring for another human life in only nine short months. We knew we couldn't go back to Atlanta without him, so we decided to give him as a gift to our newlywed friends, Scott and Janice, who had mentioned once, very casually, that they wanted a dog someday. We placed Bearfoot in a basket on their doorstep with a note that said: "Will Snuggle for Food." When our doorbell rang the next morning, we opened the door to find our sweet puppy with another note: "Will Piss and Cry for Food ALL NIGHT LONG!!!!" He's been ours ever since. We thought about calling him "Barefoot" (as in "Barefoot and Pregnant"), but we opted for the more masculine "Bearfoot" on account of his gigantic puppy feet.

At eleven years of age, Bearfoot is an old man now. Some days his arthritis gets the best of him. If you walk past him too quickly on the hardwood floors, his legs sprawl out from under him just like Bambi on ice. He tries to follow our three boys upstairs to sleep every night, but in the morning his legs buckle underneath him when he is halfway down the stairs and he slides to the bottom like a sled. Poor old Bearfoot Dog. I have begun to realize that The Doggie Without Shoes won't always be with us. I suppose that makes each day even more special when I come home from work and he greets me in the driveway with his whole-body wag and a smile. Life doesn't get much better than that.

AMY HUGHES

SAINTE ABIGAIL OF SAVANNAH ("ABBEY DODD")

My home is downtown in Savannah's historic landmark district. I am an uptown girl, but I was born on the Isle of Hope near Wormsloe Plantation. My mother and daddy live there with their owners. I have heard that my birth daddy, Pete, is a great hunter; he has been known to jump the fence and run to Wormsloe to sniff the trail of wild boars. One time he caught a young one and carried it all the way home to his house. Very impressive, but I prefer my life of luxury in the city.

Many dogs would love to have my life. I have my very own sofa in front of the television; and I am allowed to sleep on the bed with my master, take baths in the claw-foot bathtub, eat strawberries and oranges, and lick the bowl of chocolate ice cream eaten by my dad. We also go to Forsyth Park, where I play and run with the other city dogs. My father says that I am the fastest dog in the park. I tend to agree with him, but I still have not been able to catch a squirrel. Maybe some day.

My father takes me for rides in the convertible to the country to take a short break from the busy city, where I also get to chase squirrels. I always enjoy a change of scenery and running with other dogs. We visit our friends, the Potts. I get to play with Hunter, Jaeger, and Cassie, who live on the water. Very fun. I like to play with Hunter, the daddy of Jaeger and Cassie. Hunter is the top dog—the Alpha male. He pretends to be really rough and mean, but I have him doing flips and cartwheels in no time. He's a sweetie and a great protector. We have fun together. I love to visit the country, but there is no place like home.

My favorite place is the sunniest spot in the courtyard. Doggie heaven on earth. I love to lie in the cool mulch and soak up the sunshine while I smell the garden smells. I stand guard, waiting and watching for the slightest movement in my vicinity—a falling magnolia leaf, a sparrow in the bird-bottle nest above me, or a cardinal bouncing on the oleander branch hanging over my courtyard wall. I am a protector and huntress. I am a German shorthaired pointer, and I must live up to my breed.

I especially dislike lizards and must prevent them from invading my territory. I see them and, like clockwork, I rise to the occasion and ready into my pointing position with my tail straight in the air, wait until the right moment, and then *charge* . . . !

ABBEY

HUNTER
DUCKPOND
POTTS

After being asked to write a little about myself, I couldn't resist. After a long drawn-out thought process, I couldn't figure out which parts were significant to write about since everything in my life is so important. So I will start from the beginning. My father lived with my master, and they thought they wanted another puppy. They didn't realize, however, that once I was born I would break the mold forever.

When I was a puppy my curiosity was peaked every once in a while. For example, there was the time I had to investigate what the small tiny things that were swarming around my head were. Needless to say, they were not very friendly when I came into their nest. I ended up having to go to the vet and getting several shots of benadryl to stop the swelling. That wasn't the only time I visited the vet. I had to go in for surgery another time, when my curiosity peaked once again and I somehow ended up with a fish hook through my nose. The doctor had to surgically remove the hook. I may have been a little curious when I was a young pup, but I always knew I had a wonderful master. He would take me duck-hunting and fishing. When I saw him start to load the boat up to go fishing or hunting the night before, I would sleep all night in the back of the truck waiting till morning when we would leave. My dad, master, was so incredible. He could do everything—shoot ducks, catch huge fish, give great wheelbarrow rides, play ball with me for endless hours, and take me on fun jeep rides; and he always let me take naps with him to reenergize so we could move on to our next big adventure. My dad would take me everywhere with him. On one occasion we were on our way down to Butterbean to go for a swim, and I accidentally leaned a little too far outside of the truck and fell onto the pavement. But I was okay, I just had a bloody nose.

After my father died my master and my mom thought once again that it would be a good idea to have another dog. I thought it might be a good idea as well—someone I could show the ropes to, more or less someone I could show who the boss was. Most dogs only dream of being in doggie heaven. They have no idea what it is like at the Potts residence. What else could you ask for—saltwater to swim in, someone there to always throw the ball for you—and who could forget the nightly dinners of dry dog food, Alpo, and chopped-up hotdogs? Who would have imagined that Jaeger and Cassie, also known as "the terrors," would end up on our doorstep? I am their father, and quite frankly, between you and me, most of the time I can't stand to be around them. I frequently have to look down my snout at them and remind them of their place in the family, as the family pets. I constantly have to remind them of the pecking order—me at the very top and then somewhere lower on the totem pole are where they are.

My dad got sick about two years ago—he had to get a new liver—and wasn't able to take us out on the fun adventures anymore. I missed him *so much* while he was at Emory. Every day I yearned for his return until one day he arrived out of thin air. I was so excited that I think that I lost all my wits, jumping all over his feet and almost knocking him down to the ground. At first we laid around a lot waiting for him to fully recover, and then one day he was back to his normal self. We had great times once again where I would ride in the jeep next to him and we would go and do all kinds of fun stuff.

Six months later my dad got very ill and couldn't do anything with us anymore. I got to lie beside him on the floor while he stayed in the bed or I tried to sneak up onto the bed a few times to cuddle with him. He lay in bed for a long time and never got better. I was his guard dog and watched over him up until the end. I will always miss my dad; and every day I look for him, but to no avail, for he is never there. But I have wonderful and great memories of him that I will always cherish.

In dedication to the best master in the world, Darrell Potts.

HUNTER

XENA
THE WARRIOR
PRINCESS

This is Xena the Warrior Princess, the newest member of the Nash pack. Xena's family now consists of a daddy and mommy (my husband and I) and six adopted siblings: Rosie, the Rottweiler; Louie, the Corgi mix; Lola, the shrunken-down Norwegian elkhound; and three cats: Cleo, Slinky, and Lucky Stucky. Xena has only been with us for a few months, but within a few hours of her arrival in our home she had acquired the universal attitude of the other six furry pack members: "I have always lived here; I was born here; my mommy [that's me] gave birth to me here."

I found Xena dumped at the Humane Society after it had been closed. At first I couldn't believe that she had been abandoned. How could anyone cast off this nine-pound, long-haired Chihuahua-terrier mix to fend for herself? Surely she was a lost dog. But advertising brought no distraught owners to light, and long before the week was up, Xena's "bed-headed" body was firmly established in her new family.

It didn't take long to figure out what character flaws might have been less than endearing to her previous owners, for despite being taken out, let out, and pushed out about twenty times per day, Xena occasionally felt, and satisfied, the urge to anoint our living room carpet in various ways. Unfortunately no one has ever caught her in the act. So we did what any self-respecting besotted pet owners would do—we had the living room carpet replaced with easy-to-clean tile. Problem solved? Not quite.

All my dogs sleep in a small den in the kitchen wing of the house. It is a comfy, upholstered, dog-bedded, and carpeted haven at day's end. Apparently Xena never heard the dictum that dogs don't mess where they sleep. Deprived of living room carpet (she does not mess on tile), Xena found two corners of her bedroom to be a sufficient outlet. And, of course, we were still unable to catch her in the act.

I did, however, come sufficiently close to doing so that I felt justified in yelling at her. This resulted in what we now call "The Face." Upon observing The Face, as in the photo submitted with this story, most people say, "She's smiling." I beg to differ. Any loud scolding voice or even a sternly voiced command results in "The Face." I believe that what Xena is expressing to me is "I do have teeth, you know."

Fortunately for us this nine-pound Warrior Princess prefers the use of her lightning-fast tongue to her flashing fangs.

ARLENE NASH

SIMBA

Previously I had the pleasure of sharing the story of Amoco with all who perused the pages of the first *Savannah Dogs* [see pages 296–98]. Amoco passed away six weeks after the release of the book, but not before she enjoyed a little of the fame surrounding a book release. Amoco signed numerous copies for family and friends, and enjoyed every second of her fifteen minutes. I feel certain that she passed on feeling full and complete in her brief life. Of course the entire time I had to deal with the bruised ego of Simba. While his name was mentioned in the opening sentences, the story dealt solely with Amoco. I take pen in hand in an effort to remedy this slight.

Simba was a mix-breed black Lab. When I first met Simba, a young woman from South America, who lived just down the lane from my shop on Henry and Drayton streets, owned him. Probably four to five months old at the time, Simba was full of life and ready to play. He had a playmate, Demi, probably close to the same age. When the owner was not paying close attention, Simba and Demi would tear off down the lane and look in on the gang at my shop. At least the owner knew where to find her dogs.

The owner attended SCAD full-time and worked when she could, so there was not much time spent with the dogs. As both Simba and Demi were still puppies, they needed a great deal of attention. They also needed to get outside and play as much as possible. Unfortunately, with the owner's schedule this did not occur often enough. This also led, indirectly, to me taking over as the care-giver for Simba.

On a cold and blustery November morning—it was still dark out—I was opening up the shop, setting out the equipment for the day's work to come. Out of the corner of my eye I saw Demi go racing west on Duffy Lane with Simba right behind in hot pursuit. Fortunately for Demi, she made it across Drayton Street; Simba was not so lucky. A white Chevy pickup truck struck Simba just as he made Drayton Street. The impact knocked Simba into the neighbor's yard. The pickup truck stopped to assist, but there was nothing either of us could do. Simba had taken off, east on Duffy, and we would not find him for three days.

After a brief search the driver of the white Chevy truck headed on to his work and I returned to mine. Demi came back looking for Simba, but I could offer no assistance there. Simba was hurt and he was hiding, I hoped. Thirty minutes later the owner showed up looking for Simba, and I gave her the somber news. She did not believe me at first, but after several minutes the owner reconciled herself in the knowledge that Simba had indeed been struck by the truck. She started to cry and ambled toward her apartment. I was mad at her for not looking after the dogs properly, but I felt sad that Simba was hurt and lost, or maybe even worse . . .

The following morning I looked up, and there was the child of SCAD, looking a bit forlorn and quizzing me about Simba. I could only reply that I had not seen nor heard from Simba. I took it as an ominous sign, and I believe she did too. She meandered down the lane, looking left and right for any sign of Simba. Late the following afternoon my mechanic called me outside, and there stood Simba. Other than the obvious dirt on his coat, Simba did not look any worse for wear. He came toward me, tail between his legs with a sheepish smile creased across his broad face. He was okay, but badly bruised. I fed him and kept him overnight. The next day Simba was returned to the young lady from South America with a request that she carry Simba to the vet. She said that she would, but somehow I knew that she would not. A week later I ran into her and the dogs in the lane. Simba was not limping and appeared in good health. There was nothing further I could do under the circumstances.

Life has a funny way of presenting things to us —some with great fanfare and great expectations, while others just sneak under the fence. Fortunately for me, Simba was a special dog; and his entrance into my care, custody, and control was a reflection of just how special he was, at least in my opinion and hopefully yours.

Several days later the child of SCAD came running down the lane, screaming and hollering. None of us could make out a word she was saying. The gang at the station followed her to her apartment. The back door was wide open, and Simba was hiding behind the couch. When I first walked in, I thought the apartment had been burglarized. But no, the destruction was of a different sort, and it smelled. Smelled really bad. It took a few attempts to come to grip with what had exactly transpired inside the apartment, but it appeared that the owner had purchased a carpet runner for the hallway. She had left the following morning for school and work, never coming home to check on the dogs. It would appear that Simba was not appreciative of her failure to maintain his care and comfort. To show his dissatisfaction with his owner, Simba had eaten the new carpet runner. No, he didn't just tear it up, he actually ate as he could swallow. That, in and of itself, would not warrant a story, but what goes down frequently comes back up—or out in this case. And out it came all over the walls, the ceilings, and the furniture. Seems that the carpet and Simba's digestive track were not in sync. Simba was hiding behind the couch because he was embarrassed. The child of SCAD was crying, Simba was in great distress, and I was trying to keep from laughing. It was a sight to behold, but not for long. I turned to leave, but the owner handed me Simba's leash and handed me Simba. It took the ruination of the interior of her apartment to bring her to the realization that she could not properly care for Simba. Her loss was my gain and Simba's too.

At that point in time I had been dogless for nearly two years. To make matters worse, I was living in a one-bedroom apartment on Jones Street and Simba was weighing in at a hundred pounds. Not much room, but we managed. With lots of time and attention, Simba became a well-mannered and well-adjusted dog. The official "greeter" at Logan's Amoco, he knew which cars carried doggie treats and would amble out as soon as he recognized the sound of their engine. What a great dog. There are numerous stories to tell, but space prevents me from boring you all with the particulars. Simba passed away from cancer six months ago. He is sorely missed by all.

BROTHER LOGAN

BLOCKER'S BRIDGET CLAIRE ("BRIDGET")

Bridget, a small red dachshund, was born on July 16, 1992, near Macon, Georgia. She was chosen as a gift for my mother, Claire, in South Carolina, who had lost her last pet to old age and was recuperating from serious surgery. This little two-pound bundle of joy cheered up my mother and father immensely. Bridget would grab a stuffed teddy bear five times her size and run down their hall with it as if to say, "Look at me. I'm powerful." They would laugh until tears were running down their faces.

This elderly couple spoiled Miss Bridget, including the cooking of chicken-and-rice and other delicious meals for her. Bridget might eat a small amount, then they would put it up in the frig until they warmed it up for her later. Nothing was too good for Miss Bridget. She had many sweaters; and if it was the least bit chilly, she had to wear a sweater when she went out to potty.

One of my fondest memories was when my mother discovered that all of her jewelry was missing from a tray on her small ladies' dresser. We thought that

259

someone had slipped in and stolen the jewelry, but to our surprise each piece, unharmed, was in Miss Bridget's doggie bed. This little pup had really had to work hard jumping in the dresser chair so many times to take each piece of jewelry and hide it in her bed. My mother said, "Well, you know, a girl has to have her jewelry."

As the years went by, Bridget's master and mistress passed away and she came to live with me in Savannah. It was quite a change. I had four other dogs and often was fostering one or two for the Save-A-Life Animal Welfare Agency. Bridget became a neurotic, mean little cuss, biting everyone who dared to try to pat or befriend her. All of my friends were deathly afraid of this ten-pound dachsie. My friend David gave Bridget a piece of chicken that she promptly wolfed down. When he reached down to pat her, she bit his hand, drew blood. "Some appreciation," he said, and left her alone.

As the years slipped by, as they have a habit of doing, Bridget began to mellow, maybe because she was aging or had finally got used to not being the only spoiled child. Now she loves almost everyone and wants to sit on the laps of her favorite people—taking the treats without biting the hand that feeds her. She has become an outstanding Savannah dog. Of course in October she attends the annual dachshund races sponsored by the Friends of Animals, but as an observer, only because of her age and some back problems. At the races she enjoys visiting with her own kind and eats all the treats offered to her by other dachshund lovers. Bridget has become a perfect little lady and now is a pleasure to be around again. She plans to live to a ripe old age right here in her favorite city.

JULIE BLOCKER

SCOUT MURRAY

My early life began at the University of Georgia at a fraternity house. My owner left me there after I chewed up his apartment when left alone all weekend. I entertained myself at the fraternity house by harassing the mailman, cornering the pizza delivery man in the hall, and begging for food on Game Day. My best dog-friend from the adjacent house would come over every day to run and wrestle on the front lawn. My favorite toy was two-liter Coke bottles that were left in the halls.

At the fraternity house there were two brothers who began to take care of me and let me sleep in their rooms. During my first Christmas they took me to their home in Savannah even though their parents had said "no more dogs." By the end of my stay I was best friends with Mom and Dad. I continued to go back and forth between Savannah and the University of Georgia. Eventually I decided that I liked living in Savannah at Mom and Dad's house rather than at the University of Georgia.

That was six years ago and my life could not be better. At home I have my own chairs to sleep on. My parents take me for long walks when I smell everything.

Sometimes we go to River Street to walk where I bark at the ships. My favorite thing is chasing squirrels in the park, and it is my goal to catch one. I have tried many methods, but have not been successful. My best dog friends, Otis and Alice, moved to Pennsylvania several years ago; and my best people friend, John, moved last year. I have not made any new dog friends as I like people friends better than dog friends. My next-door neighbor brings me treats all the time. Sometimes I will wait on his doorstep until he comes out.

I hear Mom and Dad telling everyone that I am a wonderful, loyal, affectionate, and protective dog. Mom and Dad do not have any grandchildren yet, so I am the "granddog." My grandmother calls to see if I will come and visit her at the retirement home. When I look back at how my life started out and where I am today, I cannot believe my good fortune to have found Mom and Dad.

SCOUT

GODFREY WAYNE JAMES

I am a Savannah bulldog. I was born in Eastern North Carolina in 1995. 1 had a human who was a widow all to myself, so she spoiled me with attention. I got to sleep in her huge, soft bed with her every night. She took me for rides in the car to Wendy's and got me cheeseburgers regularly. She must have felt very sorry for me when I had to get medicine because she wrapped it up in a Snicker's bar, and I got to eat the whole thing.

One sad day she fell and had to go away. I lived by myself for about two weeks, and then a really nice couple came over to play. They must have liked me because they took me to their house to live. I was very unsure about what was happening at first, but they made me very comfortable at their house, so I thought I'd give it a try. I sure did miss Mrs. Williford though, especially since my new humans only fed me healthy food instead of cheeseburgers and candy bars.

My new humans turned out to be okay. They took me out to fun places like the park, and I got to play with other dogs and kids. I also went to the beach a lot and played with the sticks and shells, and played in the water. I didn't like the water rushing at me at first, but

I soon discovered that it was fun to get in and get wet. I loved to drink the water, but soon learned that it was a bad thing to do. I think I embarrassed my humans. Anyway, the water was too salty.

In September 1999 everyone in Savannah had to leave town because there was a hurricane named Floyd on the way. We were still living in coastal North Carolina and saw the news about Floyd and about all the traffic jams of people trying to get out of Savannah. We felt sorry for those people. A few days later Floyd passed by Savannah and came to see us instead. That was a bad storm and left quite a mess for my humans to clean up. Then everybody was feeling sorry for us.

Soon after, my humans brought home a tiny human named Anna. She must have been important because she changed our schedules quite a bit. I had to be very careful around Anna. She now is growing very quickly and has become quite a playmate for me. But I wish that she would stop grabbing my stubby tail.

Finally my human family decided to move to Savannah in 2001. I still get to go to the parks to play with other dogs and kids. And the water at the beach here is just as salty. Most people are very happy to see me here and call me "Uga" and shout "Go dawgs." I feel very much at home in this beautiful city, and now I know I really am a Savannah, Georgia, bulldog. I just don't know why people keep calling me "Uga."

GODFREY

HONEY DELMONTE

In the early spring of 2002 Max, my two-year-old Labrador pal, and I were walking the rails in Ridgeland, South Carolina. Even though we were flea-infested, we loved our outdoor home because we knew no other. This was the life. Little did we know that in a few short weeks all this would change.

I am a Savannah dog because of this fine lady Janice who drove by and offered us a lift. You bet we were anxious at first as we watched through her car windows and saw our home pass behind us. You can't imagine our excitement as we rounded the corner to Janice's house. Janice introduced us to her husband, Raymond, and to about two dozen other dogs. Their fate was also changed because they too had accepted a ride with Janice. What we were in for was some real Southern hospitality.

Janice and Raymond fed us, bathed us, tended to our flea bites, and promised that the rest of our lives would be filled with nothing but kindness, love, and full stomachs. Their home was our home. Each night we watched television together, all twenty-nine of us. Their home was filled with music that rocked us to sleep. Our days were heavenly, we romped with our new pals, nothing could be finer . . .

One Friday afternoon in June, a car pulled up and out piled a brother, sister, and mother—lonely New Englanders who had just moved to Savannah. They missed Massachusetts and had come to adopt one of us to help them fill their void. Several of us were brought to play around them—you know, to help them make their choice. Actually, we were trying to decide which one of us would adopt them.

I knew what had to be done to help those lonely faces, those accents. Knowing I had to be the chosen one, I just kept getting cuter by the minute—running, jumping, chasing. When it was time to decide, Janice and Raymond said the words for me: "Honey (that's me) is the puppy for you."

So I adopted them. For a ten-week-old, I knew I had a lot of work to do if I was going to make this a happy family. I needed a plan. I would walk them several times a day, but how? It was simple—make them think that I was difficult to house-train. That way I could get them outside, and it would be a great way for them to meet their Savannah neighbors. Everyone always stops to pet the cute puppy, me.

I would run them ragged. Their only escape from me would be to leave me home and for them to get out and explore Savannah. It gave them a chance to learn about Savannah's history and experience its way of life. The only thing left to do was to get them to slow down and relax. The Savannah summer helped me out there. It has been a couple months now that we have been a family, and I have never regretted adopting them. I am proud of them and how well trained they are.

As for Janice and Raymond, I will never forget your kindness, and I know I speak for all the abandoned dogs that you've opened your home and hearts to. Thank you for making so many families' lives so happy and complete.

Love, paws, and kisses,

HONEY

BLACKJACK, KING OF THE DECK ("JACKY" AND "SMILING JACK")

Hi. I am a four-year-old Yorkshire terrier, and I must say I am full terrier. I am a Southern dog from Charleston, at least that is where I was born. I will never forget the ride home to Savannah. Ooh, I was ever so car sick. That was not fun at all. Just to think about going for a ride makes me a little queasy. I don't understand how any dog jumps into a car, willingly. Just leave me home to guard the house.

I love to play with my brother, Caesar, the wiener dog. He occasionally tries to take my toys, but I am quick to steal them back. I have the idea that "all toys are mine." My favorites are squeak dog (squeaky hotdog) and various sizes of nerf balls. I can catch a ball on the fly, as long as my mom keeps my hair cut and out of my eyes. I play fetch, but hate to give it up without a good tug-of-war first. I am quite selfish with the blankets in the house, too. I like to chew on a blanket like a pacifier. I have two blankets that I claim for my own, but I also pull and tug blankets off my parents if I want what they have. I know they don't understand that "all blankets are mine."

My parents stopped setting the alarm clock because

268

I make such a good one. I will wake them between 5:30 and 6:30. I can't sleep my life away. I have to play. I jump and dance on mom and lick her in the face if I think she might be awake . . . or should be. I like to eat early in the morning so I can have time to play with the food dish. I eat with my Yorkie sister, Rulette. She eats from the dish that I want to eat from, even though there is a dish for her. Switching dishes is out of the question. She makes me wait, which can be so annoying. I have to be cautious. Although I am fifteen years of age, I think Rulette could take me. I bark and then run to tell my parents that she won't let me eat. When they ask me, "Are you done eating?" I run as fast as I can to dive back into the dish before they pick it up. It is usually good for a few pieces of food on the floor. I like to bat the dish around the room with my front paws to knock the food out also. The world is a game and I love to play.

I have beautiful thick hair when it grows out, but it is way too hot in our Savannah summer heat. It takes too much away from my playtime to sit for a brushing. My brother has been known to pull me by my ponytail, so I prefer to sport a short butch "doo" with a bandanna around my neck. If you come to visit, you might find me lounging on a cool spot like the newspaper or the cement fireplace ledge. Or you might find me in the window with my brother barking to greet the neighborhood. Bark! Bark!

JACKY

DIXIE CRYSTAL

Dixie Crystal is a rescue from the Humane Society. In fact, she was a television personality, starring in an Adopt-A-Pet spot. Lucky for me, she was already with me by the time the commercials ran. At first, she seemed to be a Basenji mix, but with a loud bark. After some searching, we discovered that she was a "Carolina Dog" or "Dixie Dingo." She is a descendant of dogs that followed humans across the Bering land mass thousands of years ago.

According to her tags, she has lived in Hawaii, Texas, and, of course, Savannah. With a great smile and beautiful coat, she can charm treats from anyone. Dixie Crystal always leaves behind some blond-and-white fur to remind others of her presence. When traveling in her convertible, she likes to put her head out and bark "hello" to passersby.

Ms. Crystal is a bundle of energy and loves to play in Forsyth Park at any opportunity. Dixie Crystal is as sweet as her namesake.

MARK LINSKY

GLADYS
("GLADYSPHERE")

I was born in Savannah, Georgia. My parents are Yankees from New York, but I don't mind—they feed me pretty good and let me lie on the furniture. I have a brother too. He also was born in Savannah. He's a year older and his name is Guinness [see pages 273–75]. Guinness is a good brother; he always lets me win when we wrestle, and he makes room for me on the couch. The only time Guinness gets annoyed with me is when I try to hog all the attention from Mom and Dad.

I always hear Mom and Dad talking about how cute I am. Honestly, I couldn't care less about my looks, but I do believe it keeps them from getting too angry with me when I get into trouble. You see, trouble is what really interests me. I love to get into things that I am not supposed to. Some of my very favorite things to chew are brassieres and sneakers. I also like to get into the garbage can whenever the opportunity arises. Lucky for me, Mom and Dad are very patient with me—and suckers for my cute puppy face.

A few days ago Mom and Dad told me that we are going to be moving far away from Savannah to a place called Portland, Oregon. This made me a little nervous

271

at first because I rather enjoy the warm weather plus we live right next door to Forsyth Park. Why would we leave such paradise? Then they explained to me that we are going to live right next to a park at our new house, too. And even better, at this new park there are lots of other dogs to play with; and the very best part, I don't have to wear my pesky leash. I think it is very important for dogs like me to be able to run free and play with other dogs. Maybe one day, dogs will be allowed to run without a leash in Forsyth Park.

I guess that you can say that I am pretty excited about the move. Guinness is too. I will miss a lot of things about Savannah—especially my friends, evening walks through the pretty squares, and Walls' Barbecue (Mom sneaks Guinness and me to Walls' for tastes while Dad isn't looking). But I am not sad. Mom and Dad have promised that we will come back someday for a visit, plus I cannot wait to explore a brand new city with my family. I just can't believe I will be living so far up north. Still, I'll always be a "Savannah Dog" at heart.

GLADYS

GUINNESS ("SNOUT," "GUZMAN," "GUINNAPUP")

I was born in September 2000, right around the time my future dad and mom arrived in town to go to college. The first couple of months of my life weren't that much fun. I roamed around the streets looking for food and shelter. I was dirty and had a lot of fleas. Desperately I searched for help. Two days before Thanksgiving I got some.

While standing on Barnard Street, I noticed a maroon car coming toward me. With no alternative I sat by the side of the road trying to look as cute as possible. As the car passed, my floppy ears swayed with the wind. The car came to a screeching halt and out came my new dad and mom. They fell for the-cute-puppy-by-the-side-of-the-road trick. Boy, was I thankful. Later I found out that they wouldn't have even been coming that way down Barnard Street if Mom hadn't forgotten her wallet at home. A good thing she did, for my sake. Anyway, they took me home with them. It felt great to get clean and have some food.

The next day we all got into the maroon car and headed to New York for Thanksgiving and winter break. Dad and I planned to stay with Grandma for the month. She was so surprised to meet me, maybe even a bit shocked. I couldn't figure it out at first, but then I remembered that I wasn't housebroken yet. I think that may have had something to do with Grandma's demeanor.

My first Christmas was great. There were lots of new toys under the tree for me. My favorite one was the Buddy Glow Ball. I was crazy for this ball. I chased it for hours and could hardly stop for a break.

When we got back home to Georgia, there was a bit of a problem. Dad and Mom were living in the dorms, and I was not welcome. Luckily my Uncle Jay lived in a house in upstate New York, where I would be welcome. Off I went to live with Uncle Jay until Dad could find a new place where he could live and where I would be welcome. The trip to live with Uncle Jay was so exciting, but a little scary because I had to fly all by myself. My stay at uncle Jay's was great. I met so many new friends. Everyone was in good spirits all the time, and there was a party almost every night. Uncle Jay's dog, The Dude, became my best friend; and together we joined in on the festivities.

Soon enough my dad found us a place to live. Uncle Jay took me back to Dad and Mom, and helped us move into our new friend Susan's house. After three months away, it was great to see Dad and Mom again. I felt welcome at our new home. I even got to meet some new friends, Stretch and Bruno, who became my new roommates. They showed me the ropes and were very nice to me.

Within a few months we moved to a new home by the park. A couple of months after that I got a little sister, Gladys [see pages 271–72]. It's so much fun playing with her. Together we tear up the house like two little tornadoes. Now we are all getting ready to move again. This time it's to the West Coast. I'm only two, and already I've moved around so much. It's so exciting and sure beats the street.

A hearty paw shake,

GUINNESS

HARD-HEADED HANNAH THE TRAMP OF SAVANNAH ("HANNAH")

I'm also known as "Hannah Banana Boat," "Miss Boat," "Priss Ann," "Sissy," and "Sweet Thang"—all of which I respond to.

Mom and Dad are always telling me to act more like my brother, Callahan [see pages 278–80]. So I had to write my story; it's all about competition. It all started five years ago, when I was an adoptable eight-week-old puppy in a crate at Dr. Bremer's. Most of my litter had already been adopted when my future parents brought Callahan in for his annual physical. Three hours later they came back and adopted me. I had to lay down the law immediately. So at less than five pounds, sitting in the palm of my Dad's hand, I looked up at him and barked as we pulled out of the parking lot at Dr. Bremer's. I remember Dad telling Mom it was all her fault, and he sensed I'd be a handful.

Today I am a sixty-pound Goldador (half golden retriever and half yellow Lab). I still have a face that could launch a thousand ships and don't look a day over six months (in the face anyway). I live by this motto: What's mine is mine, and what's everybody else's is mine too. I'll eat biscuits right out of Callahan's mouth. He never complains. What a wuss. I do have my limits. I don't eat from the garbage can. If it's not good enough to keep, it's not good enough for me to eat. I deserve only the best. I can even get away with stealing Callahan's pinecones. Strange habit he has. Why would you want those prickly things in your mouth? I take them from him and run, throwing them in the air just to make him chase me. My mom tells everybody I march to the beat of a different drum. W-h-a-t-e-v-e-r. I still rule the roost. I have a mind of my own and it guides me accordingly. When called by my parents, I always wait to hear my name at least three times before obeying. And if I'm outside, I wait till I hear "don't make me come over there" till I respond.

Mom and Dad sent me to summer camp this year. I was a little apprehensive, but it turned out to be great. Camp was at VSS on Eisenhower, where Dr. Shealy operated on my back left leg. I must have slept through the whole thing because I don't remember any of it. I am very stoic by nature, so the shock treatments to come were painless. I met the love of my life, and I know I'm the love of hers. Her name is Lori, and she was my physical therapist. Lori exercised me and took me for swims in the pool. I love to swim and am very good at it. Better than others of my breed, if I do say so myself. I got to spend two weeks with Lori, and we both loved it. She scratched and rubbed my belly; I'm her favorite. I'm home now, and I'm sure Lori misses me. I miss her.

I have a house to run, so I'm quite busy.

HANNAH

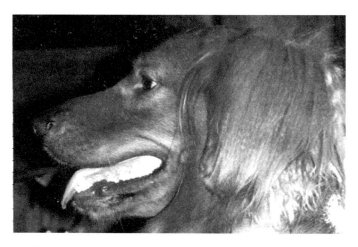

DETECTIVE DIRTY HARRY CALLAHAN ("CALLAHAN")

Woof! My name is Detective Dirty Harry Callahan—
"Callahan" to my parents and sometimes "Little Mae,"
"Monster," "Pretty Boy Floyd." I think that the title
Detective before my name must be my job description.
I'm the eldest of three siblings, fur and feathers. Being
a stud of an eight-year-old, hundred-pound golden re-
triever, I am loved by all.

Constantly on patrol, I have two lookout points. The
stairs in the dining room allow me to have full view of
the front yard and the street. From there I can alert my
family to all passersby. My second, and most favorite,
patrol spot is the backyard. I can relax a little while on
this patrol and enjoy my favorite pastime—pinecones.
I need to have at least three or four in my mouth at all
times. Sometimes I carry a tennis ball with the cones.
After hours of salivating over my cones, I shred them

one by one to the core. I know this sounds like I'm goofing off on the job, but I have the perps in the backyard well trained. While I covet my pinecones, the perps flutter and scurry around me eating the seed and corn my mom has left for them. I could be a workaholic, if only Mom would let me; day, night, winter, summer, extreme heat or cold, even rain—I love my job. You'll never hear me say, "Take this job and shove it!"

When Mom calls I reluctantly clock out and retreat to my bed in the living room. Here's the fun part. My dad is such a sucker. I can take him one of his shoes, and he knows I need (want) to take a walk. He then tells me to "go get the other one," and I obey immediately. He thinks he taught me this, but I know he needs a matching pair of shoes to walk me. Gathering pinecones on the walk is a must. I pick up as many as I can. Once home, Dad tells me to drop them. I obey. He thinks that he taught me this too, but I know Mom does not allow pinecones on the porch.

One day, while patrolling from the porch, it became very windy. All these pinecones started falling from the sky. I know God was sending me manna from Heaven. I went right through the screen to do God's will. Mom and Dad thought this a little extreme. They even called me a bad boy and said that I knew better. But, hey, it hasn't kept them from letting me patrol from the porch. I have job security.

I'm late for my shift, but I must tell you of my part-time job. Our daily walks are to the dock. At certain times of the year Dad has me herd these little blue things with really sharp claws in order to keep them from running off the dock. He calls them "crabs" and

279

catches them in big baskets. Although painful at times, I love the part-time work. I love my life and would do anything for my family.

See ya in the hood,

CALLAHAN

FIONA

That June 29th gray day started like so many others. The sky looked full of water, but who was to know it would release so much and change our lives. We left for work. The streets were dry. Fiona, our recently acquired, pound, terrier-mix puppy had been fed and toiletted, and was behind her baby gate. The day proceeded for me—teaching, making rounds, seeing patients. I didn't notice the rain beginning to fall. And fall it did; more and more in greater amounts. We had two previous floods in the house, but someone was always home to prepare, save what could be saved, and seek higher ground for man and dog.

This time it was different. I feared the worst. I left to go home around noon, just to check. What greeted me was horror as the waters rose and fear that Fiona was home alone, frightened and unable to fend for herself, or to get upstairs to safety. Six blocks from my home the flooding was remarkable. I found higher ground, parked, and put on my ever-ready waders. I sloshed through Daffin Park and waded across Waters Avenue, within two blocks of my home. The water became deeper and deeper. By the time I approached the house,

281

the water was over my shoulders (more than four feet), and walking became difficult as the water went to the feet of the waders. When I got into the house, the horror of the scene hit between my eyes. Books, furniture, mail, and debris were floating everywhere. I looked first for the baby gate; it was floating. I then called for Fiona, but there was no bark, no cry, no whimper. I waded to the stairs. The water was up beyond the third step. I looked it all over. No dog. I was dry, but terrified. I imagined the very worst: Fiona—my dog, the puppy I had rescued from the Humane Society, the white ball of fluff who was an integral family member—had perished. Fear now feigned to uncontrollable sadness. My dog was dead, drowned in the high waters of this freakish downpour.

Suddenly I heard a voice from downstairs. Outside a stranger in a rowboat called out, "Do you have a dog?" My pulse raced. Had he found her floating body? "Yes," I said with trepidation. "Well, there's a white creature bobbing up and down in your dining room. I can see it through the window." My legs brought me downstairs faster than I had ever moved. I was jolted by hitting the water again. Sure enough, bobbing, clinging to our antique high chair, now upside down, was Fiona. I reached over lots of flotsam to get her. She clung to me, literally, for dear life.

My joy and relief in finding Fiona were not sustained on account of the dire circumstances I found us in. The dog was shivering, almost crying, and I too was tearing, scared, anguished, and angry. As the waters rose higher, there was no escape. We retreated to the second floor. Since the water was surely toxic, infected by everything in its path, I washed Fiona and then myself. Windows could not open, swollen shut by the humidity. Electricity and air conditioning was all out of the question. There was still enough light to see. Then reality set in. What would we eat or drink, and how long before rescue? As luck would have it, we had matches and candles. Thus, there was light. My wife, who always stashes things in purses and carry-on bags, had left raisins, crackers, bottled water, and some candy. Thus, there was food.

I was so grateful that the dog had not perished. I was determined that she would eat and drink; I could make do for hours without nourishment. Old newspapers (a pack rat like me always has some) were available for Fiona's toilet needs. Towels were spread. We settled in for the long haul.

Although we were tired, the air was fetid, and I knew what was in store once the waters receded. I was comforted to know I had saved a life, my trusted Fiona. She cuddled, warm, clean, and soft next to me. She was truly my friend and comfort. Together we waited. An unbreakable bond between man and dog was forged.

MARTIN H. GREENBERG, M.D.

CHLOE BEIL ("PUPPY")

It all started last year. My teacher was training a dog for Canine Companions for Independence, a program in which volunteers—following the program's guidelines—raise dogs for disabled people. Anyway, my teacher, Mrs. McKernan, would bring her dog to school and the kids would help train the dog, and the dog would . . . well, train the kids. Almost everyone in my class was in love with her dog, including me. I knew I just had to have a dog.

I knew I wanted one the size of Minnie Beil [see *Savannah Dogs,* pages 352–54], now Chloe's cousin. I also knew that I wanted a dog that was trained as well as my teacher's. And if I couldn't have one as well trained, I would train it myself. I told my parents that I wanted to get a dog, and they agreed it was time to get one.

So I began my mission. I looked everywhere for dogs—on the internet, in local shelters, and even in the classifieds. My dad started taking Kate and Eric, my sister and brother, and me to the nearest Adopt-A-Pet about every week. There were small dogs, big dogs, skinny dogs, and fat dogs. Just not that perfect dog. I was beginning to think that God didn't want me to have a dog.

Then one day, when we were at Adopt-A-Pet, we saw the cutest puppies that they had just rescued. They were so small and adorable. We were actually about to get one, but then it did its business. Things took a big turn for Kate and me. The dog wasn't house-trained, of course, so my dad gave us a reminder that we would be picking up that business. And, personally, I don't want to spend my Saturday scrubbing up carpet stains. So on the way home we decided to go to one more shelter, which was a very small one. I was disappointed that I hadn't found the right dog yet, so I just stayed in the car. My brother and dad went in and came out with the prettiest dog I had ever seen. She looked exactly like Minnie. I got out of the car and went over to where they were. "Her name is Chloe," my brother said. She was so sweet. She would lie down for us to pet her, and would lick us, and she was just great. Then I asked if she could do any tricks. The lady said that she could sit, lie down, and shake hands. And, best of all, she was house-trained. Chloe was going to bring more magic to me now than I was going to bring to her. My dad said we could get her. I was so happy. I thought, This is the perfect dog.

So we took her to PETsMART and got everything she needed. She was probably beginning to think her new life was going to be great. After her shopping spree, we took her home and let her get used to the house. My mission was over. I got my dream dog.

It's been almost six months since we found Chloe, and I love her more and more every day. She is in love with my dad. She gets on the couch with him every morning. She is the best dog anyone could ever ask for.

GRETA BEIL

SHE KNEW WHAT SHE LIKED

Editor Minnie allowed me to enter the first *Savannah Dogs*, even though I never owned a dog. The reason I gave, and she bought it, was that even if I never owned a dog I still liked dogs and over the years had accumulated a few right nice dog stories. So here I am again.

Snowball is the dog I'm presenting this time. She was called that for an obvious reason—she had not the first black hair. Indeed, she was as white as a blizzard. Her breed? Well, you can speculate on that, but her owners, Harry and Bette Jennings, figured she was part spitz and part pit bull. No papers. They obtained her from the Humane Society, about six months after their previous dog died, and upon the recommendation from a neighbor who had seen her and thought she'd be just right for the Jennings.

The Jennings are friends of mine. He is a retired sea captain who, after leaving his life aboard ships, spent several years as a marine surveyor, and now is retired even from that. He was born in Liverpool, but became an American citizen many years ago. She was born in Wales, but moved to America while quite young, and has been a U.S. citizen even longer than her husband. Naturally, they are Episcopalians, and good ones at that. And by the way, they met aboard his ship; she was a passenger and he was the captain, and it didn't take him too long to ask her to marry him.

It was in their living room that I met Snowball, and we immediately became friends. Not with everyone did Snowball make such instant friends, but eventually she and the Jennings' visitors would become at least cordial to one another. I was proud that my friendship ran even deeper.

When she was a young puppy, Snowball had a pink nose (which eventually darkened), and she looked quite like a pig. Harry and Bette hadn't noticed the pig resemblance, but strangers who saw the dog immediately would say, "Looks like a pig." Darned if she didn't.

As she matured, Snowball became quite a guard dog. One incident the Jennings recall was a continuous barking one night after they had settled down for a long winter's nap. Harry woke up, spoke to the dog, and hoped that would quiet her. It didn't. She kept barking. Finally Harry got up and took the dog downstairs, opened the back door, and said, "Okay, I'll let you out." Immediately a car in his back lane cranked up, scratched off, and took off—fast. That car, Harry and Bette immediately concluded, was up to no good. At least the people in it were. But thanks to Snowball, the car left, never to return.

They have other good Snowball stories, but I think mine is best of all. It's about the dog's discriminatory love of a good drink.

I discovered this early on at the Jennings one evening as I sat by their fire with Harry and Bette, sipping a delicious Scotch and water. Harry has a way of fixing Scotch whisky just right. Not too much whisky, not too much water, and the amount of ice is just right. I noticed that Snowball ate a piece of ice Harry had taken from his glass. Then the dog looked at me.

Somehow I knew what he wanted, so I removed a piece of ice from my glass and the dog hustled over, took it, and ate it. At the time I figured he simply liked ice, but that wasn't what it was. He liked ice from a glass of Scotch.

There was another person sitting next me, a lady drinking some kind of gin concoction. She was fascinated that Snowball had consumed two ice cubes, so she took one from her glass, summoned Snowball over, and gave him the cube.

Pa-tooie! Not only did Snowball immediately spit out the ice, he snarled and made a funny noise. I called him back to me, gave him an ice cube, and he quickly ate it. Harry gave him one too. Another person in the room, who wasn't drinking Scotch, called him over and gave him a cube, and Snowball instantly spat the cube onto the floor.

Harry and I immediately figured it out—Snowball liked Scotch, and nothing else. And from then on, it was like that every time I was at the Jennings' house. Nothing but Scotch-flavored ice for Snowball.

Snowball lived eleven years, but finally was put to sleep because of a tumor. But one thing's certain—Scotch had nothing to do with Snowball's tumor. Indeed, Harry and I still drink Scotch, and neither of us has a tumor.　　　　　　　　　　TOM COFFEY